S0-BYM-353

Wild Rivers
and
Mountain Trails

Wild Rivers
and
Mountain Trails

Don Ian Smith

Illustrated by Roy Wallace

Copyright © 1985 Don Ian Smith
Copyright © 1972 Abingdon Press

High Country Books
1559 South Five Mile Road
Boise, Idaho 83709

First Edition
THIRD PRINTING

All rights reserved. No part of this book may be re-
produced or transmitted in any form without permission
in writing from the author, except by a reviewer who
wishes to quote brief passages in connection with a
review in magazine or newspaper.

Library of Congress Catalog Card Number:
85-60310

ISBN 0-932773-01-X (previously published by
Abingdon under ISBN 0-687-45536-7)

Scripture quotations noted RSV are from the Revised
Standard Version of the Bible, copyrighted 1946, 1952,
1971, 1973 by the Division of Christian Education.
National Council of Churches, and are used by permission.

Cover Photograph by Garrett Photography
Boise, Idaho.

PRINTED AND BOUND BY MAVERICK PUBLICATIONS
BEND, OREGON, UNITED STATES OF AMERICA

*To my good friend F. E. "Gene" Powers,
U.S. Forest Service; naturalist, conservation-
ist, dedicated forester, and ideal camping
companion.*

Contents

Wild River

My Christian faith has been nurtured in the mountains of central Idaho, some of the most rugged mountains in North America. The mountains have been my home; they have sheltered me from winter winds and provided me with cool water on hot summer days. I have found God out-of-doors as truly as I have ever found him in a church. Great canyon walls have been my altars, and in vast forests of fir, pine, and spruce I have known that "the Lord is in his holy temple: let all the earth keep silence before him." I have walked softly on the carpet of pine needles and breathed the incense of pure, untainted air, sweetened with the scent and oxygen from a million trees in a healthy young forest.

I have pushed back into areas so far from roads that man has been unable to manage the forest. Here trees have died of old age, as all trees will. They have fallen into tangles that have choked new growth and blocked the trails, making it impossible for game animals to make use of the area. These old dead trees have been breeding places for tree-killing insects, and they have waited for nature's way of clearing and renewing a forest —devastating fires. Lack of management can be as destructive as bad management, though we see less of it because the bad management practices have occurred nearer the places where we live.

As the population grows and we become more aware of pollution in our environment, we hear more and more about wilderness areas and wild rivers. Caught in our urban problems, we long for the free, uninhibited life that is symbolized by our remaining untamed lands. It is good that we are concerned with keeping some fresh, clean spots on earth. But it is also important to realize that the challenge of keeping such places can be met only with management, not with emotion. Man has been given dominion over the earth, and he cannot escape this obligation by trying to give great areas back to nature. Having dominion does not mean that we have to destroy; the earth is our home and we must be good housekeepers. Nature is not always a good housekeeper, and the well-intentioned urge to seal off great areas of land and certain great streams and remove them from effective management so we can have them forever primitive isn't realistic. To keep our home we must care for all of it, including our wild rivers and our wilderness lands. There is no room for a sealed-off Sunday parlor.

The fact that man has often managed his environment badly in past years does not justify a kind of nature-worship that assumes that nature can do a better job in the future. Unmanaged, nature permits game herds to expand to the point of destroying their forage and range; insects are permitted to kill great stands of timber; and nature's great cleanser—fire—is something we really cannot afford in the way in which, in past centuries, it ravaged the forests that we need for timber and recreation. It is my conviction that man can intelligently manage his land so that we can have forests with sustained yields, rivers that stay clean, and wild game that can thrive in numbers consistent with what the land will support. And we cannot have this by abdicating man's responsibility to have dominion over the earth. We can have it by accepting responsibility and applying our knowledge of management practices.

A wild river should not mean a river that is not

used, but a river that is kept clean. In this sense it seems to me a wild river is a symbol of what the Christian life should be—a thing of beauty and delight, serving those who come in contact with it, bringing a man hope and joy, being in close contact with the world and the things of the world, and yet not letting the evil of the world taint and pollute it. God has given man a will and a mind; surely a river can serve man and be kept clean and unpolluted even as a life can be of service and still be pure in itself. Surely streams that now are polluted can be converted, cleaned up, and made pure again, even as lives can be revitalized and purified even if they have once been tainted with evil. Wild rivers to me are symbols of hope—not the hope that something pure can be kept so in a sort of return to Eden, but the hope that man can manage his environment and his life with the help of God. Many of our loveliest wild rivers today once ran brown with the mud of long-dead placer mines. Surely many of our now dirty rivers can again run pure, if we will it so. And no human life can hope to stay in some state of original innocence and purity, but every life can have the hope of running pure and clean like a wild river, if there is the will to use the wisdom and the strength that God gives us.

Being deeply concerned about the need to clean up the polluted areas in our environment and keep clean the areas that are still clean, and being dedicated to the promotion of the spiritual values in our common life together, I see a close relationship between these two great interests in my life. The living of a Christian life seems to me to be very much like my association with a wild river, the Salmon River of central Idaho. A life, like a river, keeps its appeal, its beauty, its joy, by being kept clean and pure. What we would call good self-discipline and moral standards in a life we might call good management practice in the drainage of a river. In either case, it takes an effort, a dedication, a concern, but the rewards are more than ample. A life well lived with Christian faith and discipline brings a sense of joy to all who come in contact with it, just as the crystal waters, the ample wild-life, the rush and freedom of the rapids in a wild river can bring a sense of satisfaction and a deep soul-stirring to one who is blessed by contact with such a river.

As I seek to share with my readers some of my personal faith and some of the experiences that have enriched my life, I can think of no better symbolism than the comparison of the Christian life as it moves, rejoicing along its earthly course, with the flow of a clear wild river as it flows through the hills and pours out its blessing of life-giving water to the thirsty downstream lands. So I have gathered these thoughts together under the title *Wild Rivers and Mountain Trails.*

Snakes
and Butterflies

Since earliest childhood I have lived in open
country, or near enough to it that a brief walk
or a very short trip by car could put me into
open fields or brushland or mountains where the
hand of God is more evident than the hand of man.
One of my vivid memories, as I recall my childhood,
is a day when we had just moved to a new farm and

I was wandering about it, exploring, and touching, smelling, hearing, and enjoying every bit of it. There was a drainage ditch along one side of the farm. I remember picking up the feather of a wild duck, a duck that had probably nested in the cat-tails along the ditch bank. Holding the feather in my hand, I sat for a long time, just thinking— thinking about where the duck lived, where it came from, why it liked the water, and all the wonder and mystery that can come to the mind of a six-year-old boy as he holds the feather of a wild duck in his hand.

One marvel that never ceases to bring back all my boyhood sense of wonder is the dried, shed skin of a snake. I suppose I have seen hundreds of them, but I never see one without wanting to pause and reflect on the wonder of a creation that can give an ordinary, slithery snake a new skin, a couple of sizes larger, when his old skin gets too tight for him. What a miracle! And of course, for the snake, getting a new skin means getting a whole new life. I like to think about it from the snake's point of view. Here he is. His skin is getting too tight. He can't get around like he should. He can't hunt like he used to. He is frustrated and literally "uptight." Then wonder of wonders, a power he does not understand, a force beyond his wildest dreams and hope, gentle but forceful, helps him slip out of the skin that held him back and hampered his actions and frustrated his hopes. And he finds himself set free, a new creature.

As I walk through the hills looking at wild

15

flowers, or rocks, or tracks of animals, I don't see the snake but I find the old cast-off skin. Now it is just an empty, almost transparent bit of organic material, soon to return to the dust. But it tells the story, the story of a transformation, a gift of new life. And as I ponder the empty snake skin, I ponder the wonder of a power that can make all things new. I wonder why I have ever allowed myself to feel that a situation was hopeless just because I couldn't, at the moment, with my limited talent and short-sighted view of life, see my way out of some frustrating, discouraging situation that seemed to limit my life and block my efforts to achieve. Is it really so hard to believe that a God who can give a lowly snake a new skin can also give to a sinner a new life? Is it so hard to believe that he can give the hopeless new hope, the frustrated a new direction and sense of purpose? We've all heard the old pessimistic line, "You can't change human nature." Of course you can't—but God can. A snake can't change his skin, but a Creator who has done all things well to provide for his creatures, can and does.

It is interesting how one's thoughts can jump from an old snake skin under a sagebrush to a great line in the New Testament. And you think of Paul, marveling in the new power and wonder of his life, his new faith, his new hope; being able to explain it only by saying, "I have put off the old man and put on the new man and become a new creature." Now a path that seemed too dark is suddenly lighted, a job that seemed too monotonous suddenly takes on purpose, love that had died suddenly comes to life again. So simple, yet so wonderful!

Butterflies fascinate me. I understand that the name "butterfly" comes from the fact that someone once got mixed up and meant to say "flutter by," because that's what they do. But there is a fascination in a brightly colored butterfly. I like to watch him and think of the time when he was a creepy, crawly caterpillar that had to hide under a leaf when a bird came along. He looked at the bird with envy and thought what a wonderful thing it would be if he could just float through the air and let the breeze carry him about, a bright spot in the world instead of a frightened, hairy worm. And of course, one of his old pessimistic pals said to him: "You know, you can't change caterpillar nature." How discouraged he must have been, looking up at the wonder of the sky and feeling that it could not be for him because he was bound by the limitations of his worminess.

And then one day it happened. The cocoon he wound around himself to hide his ugliness and despair broke open, and when he tried to wiggle he didn't wiggle at all. He spread his lovely wings and the morning sun touched the colors. The light breeze picked him up, and there he was, floating along like a bird, rising up toward the blue of the sky—a thing of beauty. A strange power touched his life and brought beauty and a new dimension of living. He soars where he used to creep; he is a new creature with a new life.

When one sees that even a snake can have a new skin and a caterpillar can become a butterfly, is it any wonder that Jesus chided his followers a bit when they were pessimistic about their own lives and told them that they didn't trust enough. Even a human father, with all his limitations, will not give his son a stone when he asks for bread or a serpent when he asks for a fish. What wonders are in store for the one who really puts his life in the hands of God—God who not only sees a sparrow fall, but can give a new skin to a lowly snake when his old skin gets too tight, and will give a fearful caterpillar a set of wings that lift him up to the sky and make him as lovely to look upon as a falling maple leaf in the autumn sunshine.

We all live in a world that is constantly putting limitations, restrictions, and frustrations upon us; there are times when we feel a desperate need to break out of the bonds of our human weakness and rise above our smallness. Our own strength is not enough; and there are times when we are as trapped as a snake in an outgrown skin. And this is just the time when we need to remember one who says, "Behold, I make all things new," and has the ability to back up his promise.

Yard Lights and Stars

I grew up on a farm near the Snake River in southern Idaho. The Snake River plain seems rather flat, but actually it slopes up gently to the north and south to hills on either side. When one looks out toward the horizon, even though the earth is round, one does not find himself looking down around the curvature of the earth but up slightly toward the sky that is above the hills.

One of my chores, as a boy, was to feed and milk some cows. Often in winter when I was late with my chores, I found myself going out to feed the cows long after dark. I had to climb up on a tall haystack and throw hay down for the cows. One of my favorite pastimes was to take a rest, sitting in the sweet-smelling hay, and from my vantage point on the high haystack, simply look out across the vast Snake River plain. At that time the country was covered by small farms, and almost every farm, like ours, had a yard light. For miles and miles I could see the yard lights and think about them— how each light represented a farm family, and per- haps near each light someone like myself was out doing his chores.

But then, as I looked farther and farther, an interesting thing happened: the land sloped gently up toward the hills, the sky came down to meet the earth. On a clear night when the sky was filled with stars, there was always a line where I could not be sure whether I was looking at stars or yard lights. I think it was at this time in life that my interest in religion really began. I would sit there at night and ask myself, Where do the yard lights end and the stars begin? Just where does man's creation meet God's creation? I was never quite sure; and to this day I believe this is one of the most interesting questions we can face but a question we cannot answer. Quite often what we think is man-made light may very well turn out to be one of God's stars.

Certainly there are times when we as men are

expected to do things that God leaves for us to do. And blessed is the man who has learned that we cannot draw a sharp line between the work of God and the work of man saying, this is man's doing and God's help is not needed. Nor can we say, What's the use of man trying to improve his world? After all, it is in the hands of God. Surely God as a wise Father has given us much to do and expects us to work with him; but also he works with us. There are many times in life when we will not be able to say for sure where the yard lights end and the stars begin.

How true this is in the matter of healing. One has a heart attack. He calls a good doctor and says his prayers and recovers. So someone say, "What a wonder that modern medicine can do so much to heal." And certainly the medicine did help to make the healing possible. But on the other hand someone else may say, "It is a miracle that you recovered so well from your heart attack. You surely must have had an answer to your prayers." And who can say for sure just what part of the healing was from man and what part from God? Actually, there is nothing that man can do to heal an injury except to make the circumstances right for the slow and steady processes of God to do their work. If you cut your finger you cannot make it mend. All you can do is keep it clean, keep out infection, and then wait with patience for the natural process of healing, which is God's own doing.

Just where do the yard lights end and the stars begin? Who can say for sure? Very often what we think may be our own work may simply be God working through us. And surely there are many times in life when God expects his work to be done by us; unless we do our duty his work is neglected. In many of the wonderful things that happen in life it is important for us to see that the work of man and the work of God cannot be sharply separated. As we reach up in faith for the help of God, he reaches down in compassion and love to help us, and his light and our light shine together so that one cannot say which is which.

Today we are thankful for wonderful discoveries that have been made, and we give to great scientists the honor that is due them. But when a fine human mind develops a wonder drug like penicillin from a common substance like mold, it is interesting to ask: Who created the molds, and who created the mind of man, and who made men care enough about each other so they would give long hours in the laboratory to find life-giving substances? Where do the yard lights end and the stars begin?

If one believes that God created the world in six days, or if one believes he created the world in a billion years, or if one believes, as I do, that the process of creation is still going on and is an everlasting process, does it change one bit the fact that it is God who is doing the creating? Does it change one bit the part that God has in it and the part that man has in it? Does it bring us any closer to being able to live without him? Have we come any nearer to saying that man's yard lights can outshine the stars of God?

I remember a visit I once had with a little boy about six years old. He had built a very nice little toy city out of blocks that were made from scraps of lumber, the ends of two-by-fours and two-by-sixes. His work was very good, and when I praised him on how well he had built his little city he said proudly, "I did it all by myself without any help at all." And so he had, except that it was his father who had lovingly and carefully shaped the blocks and given them to him; it was his father who had provided him with a level floor in his playroom where such a structure of blocks could be put together; it was his father who had given him a home in which to work. And if we are honest we begin to see that all of man's achievements are a good deal like the little city built by the little boy— good work, but all done with the things the Father has given us and in the situation the Father has provided for us. Fortunate is the man who can make great achievements of his own and still remember to give thanks for a loving God who has given to man all the elements and wonders of the world with which to work.

The truly wise man is the humble man who knows that without the gifts of God, man could in fact accomplish nothing. And it seems to me that it is a good thing once in awhile to look out across one of our Idaho valleys on a starlit night and ask ourselves just where do the yard lights end and the stars begin. Just what part of our achievement is to be credited to the wisdom of men and just what part is the free gift of a living God?

Surely we will come away from such an experience saying, as we behold many of the wonders and blessings of life: "This is the Lord's doing, and it is wonderful in our eyes," even while we are seeking to do more and more in our effort to make this world a better place in which to live.

The Slothful Hunter

Several years ago some friends and I had a hunting camp near a forest road. We were sitting in our camp after the evening meal, when some out-of-state hunters who were camped near us stopped in for a visit. Our talk turned to different types of guns. They mentioned killing an elk that afternoon with a rather special rifle that was of interest to one of my companions, who was a gunsmith. On an impulse he said, "Could we go out and see the elk you shot and see the effect of your bullet?" So we took our gas lanterns, jumped in our pickup truck, and drove out a few miles along the ridge road to the place where the elk had been killed.

Just off the road at the edge of the timber, we found the elk. It was a fine animal with a good set of horns. But to our utter amazement no effort had been made to dress out the animal. It had been shot several times, badly smashed up, and then left just as it had fallen. We asked why it had not been cleaned; the reply was simply that they thought it would be all right to let it wait till morning. We disagreed and helped them care for the meat. As we did so, the real reason why the elk had not been dressed became evident. They didn't really care about the meat. And I'm sure that if they did try to eat some of it later, the meat would not have been very good. It had already been neglected too long.

Here were some hunters who had captured a real prize, then failed to make anything worthwhile out of it, at least from the point of view of one whose family likes good elk meat. I was reminded of a bit of wisdom from Proverbs 12:27: "The slothful man roasteth not that which he took in hunting." Many times since that experience I have reflected on the proverb and noticed other ways in which it applies to much of our modern way of living.

The old bedtime stories often began by saying, "Once upon a time a young man went out to seek his fortune." This is a good expression. In a very real sense we are all hunters, seeking meaning, or purpose, or fortune, or satisfaction in life. And one of the strange things about life in modern America is that in many ways it is easier to find a fortune than it is to make something worthwhile out of it. Finding game often is not as hard as dressing it, cutting it, preparing it, and making it into something worthwhile that will feed us and nourish us; finding success is not as hard as using it in a way that will feed the mind and satisfy the soul. All to often we are like the slothful hunter—we take something good in life but fail to roast it.

In days past we used to speak of good fortune in terms of finding a gold mine, but not any more. I have a small interest in a little mine, and I know from experience that there is quite a bit of gold in it. Some old-timers made a living digging the gold. But today, with the high cost of mining, compared with the price of gold, one cannot operate the mine. It is interesting that in Idaho today, it is easier to find a gold mine than it is to mine it. When I meet a prospector I am inclined to chuckle and ask, "What would you do with a mine if you found one?" Usually the happy prospector will admit that he hasn't the slightest idea.

In a way this illustrates an interesting fact about our modern society. We are searching for something to want. It is easier to find our fortune than it is to make something good of it; it is easier to make a living than to make a life. Some real tragedies of our time are in the lives of those who

27

have found their prizes quite easily, and then lacked the ability, or faith, or staying power to cook what they caught, to appreciate what they found.

Our being more interested in getting things than in using them well was a concern of Jesus. One of his most moving stories illustrates it. In the twelfth chapter of Luke, he tells of a man who had much good land and good harvests. So the man kept building bigger barns in which to store his goods. And just when he was planning the biggest barn of all, God said, "This night your soul shall be required of you, and then whose shall all these things be?"

One of the depressing things that a teacher runs into is the number of students who are much more interested in getting a diploma than they are in getting an education. A degree, or diploma, like a set of elk horns, has become a prize, or trophy. And many students seem to want only the trophy and have little regard for the real meat of a good education; they seem indifferent to the satisfaction that can come from learning for the sake of learning, the joy that comes simply from improving one's mind, regardless of the kind of work that he intends to do. It is discouraging to talk to a student who is interested in graduating and getting a degree, but who is not really interested in learning about government, history, or literature, or much of anything else. It seems we like catching the fish but we want someone else to clean them.

This same problem shows up in modern marriage.

Our society has associated happiness and success with a good marriage more than with anything else. Certainly there is a relationship between success and a good marriage. But often, when we talk to a girl and she says, "I just want to find happiness," she means she wants her prince charming to come along in a late model sports car and carry her away to where they will live happily ever after. There is little thought about the four-letter words like give, work, pray, hope, wait, love, that are so important if the marriage is really going to produce the happiness that the lovers desire.

The writer of a short story has a real advantage over the marriage counselor. He can tell his story, have the couple get married, and then assume their happiness without ever checking up to see if it really happens that way. In life it isn't so simple. What happens after the wedding, in terms of work, sharing, and striving, is more important than just finding the right mate. Our society puts far too much importance on the chase and not nearly enough importance on what one does with a mate after he or she is captured. As one reads the magazines and sees the TV commercials, he gets the idea that for a young woman the process is something like that of the trophy hunter—the object is to catch the man, tag him with a marriage license, and boast about the prize. There is little emphasis on the need for loving, cherishing, sharing, giving, and forgiving that have to go into the making of a home, if the affection that has been captured is really going to be a blessing in one's life.

It is a wonderful thing to have a membership in a church where one can worship and find food for his soul. Certainly many are finding great satisfaction in being part of a church. But there are church members who have not found satisfaction in being part of the church. It was easy for them to join; they were glad to have their name on a roll book. But then they failed to do the work that is necessary to make a church membership into a fellowship that can enrich life. Like the slothful hunter they have been content with capturing the prize of a church membership, but they have not bothered to make it into something that can feed and nourish their spirit. They have found a wonderful resource but have not made it into something of real value because they have not been willing to work at it.

It is often easier to find our fortune than it is to use it wisely. In terms of our work, our marriage, our education, our church, or other areas of life, we must beware that we are not like the slothful man who does not roast what he takes in hunting.

To Corner a Toad

It is always sad to see someone who fails to live up to the best of which he is capable. I remember a fine little dog that I had on our ranch. She was a pretty good watchdog most of the time, but she had a problem with her sense of values.

I remember one night she was making a great fuss—her voice was so urgent, her barking so sharp, that I was sure there was a bear out in the yard causing some trouble. I took my rifle and a light and hurried out to see just what was causing all the commotion. And there was my faithful dog with a large toad backed into a corner. There is something pretty sad about a good watchdog, well-bred and well-fed, giving her all just to corner a toad. Sometimes when I see the things to which capable, talented people give the best years of their lives, I am reminded of the dog that made just as much fuss over a toad as a bear. Sadly enough, this is a picture of life for too many of us in America today.

Long ago the prophet Isaiah saw this problem among people of his time and cried out, saying, "Why do you spend your money for that which is not bread, and your labor for that which does not satisfy?" The reason we do is because we fail to set real, worthwhile goals in life; we lack a standard of values that will keep us on the course we want to take for all the years of our lives. A person's life is like a good story, or a good symphony. It can have many variations but it needs a central theme running through it, a theme that sets the tone of the life and gives it a sense of purpose and value.

This is what a firm Christian faith does for the life of the individual. The apostle Paul called this singleness of mind. It doesn't mean being narrow-minded, but it does mean having a definite reason for living. It is what Jesus called the narrow way that leads to life, as compared with the broad and easy way that leads to nothingness and a wasted life. Paul put it like this: "But one thing I do, forgetting what lies behind and straining forward to what lies ahead, I press on toward the goal for the prize of the upward call of God in Christ Jesus our Lord".

Paul did a lot of things. He was one of the most active men in history. He was a tentmaker by trade—a good one. He could have made his living in this way and said, "My tent business is so good I don't have time for the church." But he made tents, and was also a great preacher, teacher, writer, and traveler, having to do most of his traveling on foot. But he never let all his various activities sidetrack him from his main purpose, which was to be a good Christian—a true follower of Christ. He kept this one great goal always in mind, and this theme of his life made all the other activities make sense. It put them in their proper places. His great theme was not to make a living but to live a great life; making a living was simply one of his activities. His aim was a life that was pleasing in the sight of God. A life pleasing to God does not need to contradict a life that is pleasing to men. In the long run, the only way to live a really great life in the sight of men is to be sure it is a life that is pleasing in the sight of God. But pleasing men cannot always be a sure way of pleasing God.

We are free to choose the course we take in life. To make a wise choice we need some standards and values that come from our Christian faith. Over and over Jesus stressed the need for singleness of mind. It isn't always easy to stay with our good intentions. It's easy to rationalize.

I once read about a hound that had a tempermental defect. No matter how hard his master tried to train him, he would never get over his one great problem of not keeping on the track of the animal he was supposed to chase. The hound would start out, as he was supposed to, on a lion track; he would run the lion until it was almost ready to go up a tree. Then he would cut a deer track, and, forgetting the lion, he would go in pursuit of the deer. But before catching the deer, he would become interested in the track of a fox, and after chasing the fox until it was about ready to give up, he would take off in pursuit of a rabbit. To make a long story short, this fine dog, that had the ability to be a good lion hound, would start the day in pursuit of a lion, but after a long hard day of running, he would end up with a chipmunk up a tree. He had never learned that to attain certain goals in life, one must set his heart and mind on one goal and stick with it.

This matter of getting sidetracked from our goals in life is something we all have to watch for. It is easy to do. We get to thinking that if something takes our time, it must be important. It might be that if we are really honest in our evaluation, we will find that much of our time is being spent on chasing toads.

Sometimes we find it easier to chase toads because we don't have the spiritual courage to chase anything bigger. Our toad hunts are excuses for our lack of courage. It is easy to be like the man who heard that there was a bear after his stock up in the north pasture. So he began to make preparations to go after the bear. He oiled his gun, took extra flashlight batteries, packed a lunch, oiled his boots; in fact, he took enough time getting ready to go after the bear that he could be very sure it would be gone by the time he got there.

Some of us have a way of doing this in life. We can act pretty important and make big plans —plans so big that they become an excuse for not doing anything at all about the need that is right next to us in the place where we live. We find enough toads to chase to keep us very busy until the real jobs that need to be done have been done by someone else or left undone.

There are many real jobs that need to be done and problems that need to be solved in our own homes, our own towns, our own churches. We each have twenty-four hours in a day and seven days in a week. We need to see how we are spending these precious hours which add up to lives. We need to watch out for toads that seem to need chasing but would be just as well left alone while we pursue some more important causes.

It is amazing how we can give time to trivial things that take time out of all proportion to what they are worth. I know it is dangerous to be specific, but at the risk of offending someone I will be specific about one matter: the matter of meetings that we attend where nothing happens, meetings that take time that would be better spent at home with our children, or in Christian fellowship with someone who is lonely. So many of our meetings are not only pointless, they are not even fun. We hurry to go to a meeting held only because people like ourselves have hurried to get there. Take a close look at the meetings that are taking up your important time. What is really happening at these meetings? Some, of course, are very important. But if a meeting has done nothing to bring you closer to your fellow man or closer to God, or has done nothing to enrich your life and the life of your community, the chances are you have been on a toad hunt.

We do spend our days, just like we spend money. But there is no way to earn more days. We indicate this in our language when we say: I spent the day in town, or I spent the day at work, or I spent the summer at summer school. The fact that we spend our days is something we can do nothing about. We have to spend them. But we can decide what we will spend them for. It would be a tragic thing if we came down to the end of our days and found we had spent our good days and bought only dust and ashes. What a joy it is to come to the end of our days knowing we have spent them for those things which do bring us closer to God and to our brothers, to find that we have stayed with our high calling and captured a true prize, and have not spent our time putting a toad in a corner.

Lost and Found

Quite a few years ago two elk hunters were lost in the wilderness on the north slope of the Salmon River canyon. It is an interesting area. The stream on which they were hunting runs for about twenty-five miles from the divide between the Salmon drainage and the Bitterroot drainage. The stream goes from an elevation of about nine thousand

feet, down to the main Salmon River and an elevation of about thirty-five hundred feet. There are no
roads in the immediate area where the hunters were
lost, but a forest service road runs along the divide
at the head of the drainage, giving access to several
forest service fire lookout stations. A good trail runs
along the main Salmon River.

From the point where the hunters became lost
they could have gone uphill and found the forest
service road, or they could have gone downhill
and found the trail along the river. But for five
days they were lost. Concerned outdoorsmen, men
from the Forest Service, and some from the Fish
and Game Department joined in the search. The
weather was cold; there were snowstorms. Each day
the searchers found abandoned campfires and tracks
in the snow, but for five days they were not able
to come upon the lost men. In their frantic efforts
to save themselves the lost men eluded the search
parties; they made it very difficult for those who
knew the way to find them. After the search was
officially abandoned, one dedicated Ranger continued the effort and finally came upon the lost
men; except for his dedication the hunters would
have perished.

Asked why they had continued to wander when
a definite effort going uphill would have taken
them to the forest road, or a long walk downhill
would have taken them to the trail along the river,
they said they had discussed the situation, realized
this was a possibility, and had made a practice
of going uphill half a day and downhill half a day.

To one who is used to the mountains and knows the vastness of the area involved, this answer seems so foolish that it seems impossible. But frightened people do foolish things. The fear of death by exposure can bring on a panic which can upset all reason. It is a common saying among us who enjoy the mountains that no man is lost until he has lost his head. He may get mixed up in his directions; he may go the long way around to get back to camp. But real lostness is a frame of mind, not a physical situation.

The interesting part of this incident is the fact that the confused, frantic effort of the lost men to save themselves was the very factor that made it impossible for the searchers to find them. Had they recognized this, stayed by their campfire, and trusted the searchers, they would have been found soon after the officials organized the search.

As a family we have always enjoyed the out-of-doors and spent time camping in remote areas. When our children were small we recognized the danger of lostness for a child who wanders away from camp in a forest area. Realizing this is a very real danger, we had what we called "lostness drills" for our children, even as a school has fire drills so that the children would know what to do if a real danger arose.

If the children became lost, their first rule was to stop wandering and wait. They could sing if they felt like it, or they were to find a log and drum on it with a stick, pretending to be primitives giving drumbeat messages. Obviously, we wanted them to make sounds so we could find them. But their basic instruction was to stay in one place. They were to make themselves as comfortable as possible, then wait and trust. Over and over we gave them the assurance that if they were lost, because of our love for them, they could be sure that we would never give up searching until we found them. And above all, they should not make the search harder by continuing to wander without knowing the way. If they were lost, they would not need to know the way back to camp; they would need to have confidence in their father's love and be trusting enough to wait for him to find them.

In a sense this is the very heart of the good news of the Christian gospel. There are certainly many different kinds of lostness in our time. The least of our dangers is that of being literally lost in a wilderness. But what person does not find, in some area of his life, a sense of lostness in terms of finding meaning, or relating to other people, or in facing up to the great problem of aging, and finally making the great step we all must make through the valley of the shadow called death? One of the greatest mistakes most of us make is that we read the wonderful story Jesus told about a lost sheep and think of ourselves as among the ninety-nine that were safe. But Jesus wasn't talking about the ninety-nine. They are just props in the story to make evident the plight of the one that is lost. The lost sheep is every man.

The wonder of the gospel is the news that we have a Shepherd who will not give up the search until the lost is found. The sad part for many of us is that we, either in panic or overconfidence in our ability to save ourselves, keep running frantically, up for half a day and down for half a day, never waiting in simple trust long enough to give the one who knows the way a chance to find us. Ours is not a hidden God who must be discovered by our human questing. Ours is a Father who yearns for his alienated son, a Shepherd who never gives up his search for the sheep that is lost, and rejoices when he finds it.

Fear Not

Living for many years in central Idaho near the
Salmon River wilderness country, I have had some
contact with the problem of searching for people
who get lost in the rugged mountains of that area.
Lost hunters are a rather common problem, and
many men have to take time to go in search of the
lost people.

As one becomes more aware of the problem, he realizes that the real danger that comes to a lost hunter or hiker is not the danger of being out in the hills alone. Many people live out in those hills alone all the time. The danger is fear. Fear is a much greater danger than hunger, or thirst, or exposure. In the situations I can remember, a hunter was never killed by exposure where there was not first of all fear, panic, unreasoning fright, causing the person to use up his energy unwisely, or to injure himself trying to run through rough country. And in so many situations in life, fear is our enemy. Fear of illness is often worse than illness itself. Fear of cancer can cause as much damage as cancer does; fear of poverty plagues people as much as poverty. And confidence, or faith, can be a real, saving force.

Just recently, some people I know were bringing a jet boat up the Salmon River. They were caught in slush ice that had formed what is called an "ice bridge" across the river. Slush ice is not solid enough to walk on, but it can stall a boat and ice up the jet so the boat loses its power. Many people in this situation would have allowed fear to destroy them. But the people involved, confident in their ability to handle the situation, were not in great danger. They made a sort of snowshoe raft out of oars and life jackets, and safely got across the slush ice to shore. Fear could easily have killed them; confidence saved them. They had faith in their ability to solve the problem wisely.

The world in which we live is filled with situations where fear can destroy and faith can save. Fear is one of the greatest enemies that we face in life. In fact, fear is more of an enemy than death; it is our fear of death that causes our trouble, much more than death itself. And to our fear, the Christian faith speaks a clear word: Fear not, I have good news for you. God cares! He sees a sparrow fall, and you are worth far more than a sparrow. Let not your heart be troubled.

In medicine we often speak of the crippling diseases: polio, arthritis, rheumatism, and others. And surely these can cripple us in terms of physical action. But of all the things that cripple, nothing cripples like fear. Fear can keep us from doing many things we ought to do, and it can cause us to do foolish things we ought not to do. We remember the story of the talents. The man who did not use his money, but buried it uselessly in the ground, was asked why he did not invest it or do something with it. And his answer was simply: "I was afraid."

How often in life we meet failures. And when we check on the cause of the failure, it is simply this same old statement: "I was afraid." The opposite of fear is faith; faith sets us free for action. It is a very interesting thing to note that in life, our worst fears come when we are lying down thinking about them. They begin to go away when we get up and get into action, when we do something about the problem that bothers us.

Many of us are terribly handicapped by our fears. We need to learn that fear vanishes when we get up

44

and do something about it. I remember once when I was out camping, I heard what I was sure was a bear, just outside my tent. He was grubbing and sniffing around. For some time I lay in fear, wondering just what I should do. It seemed like he was getting closer and closer. And when it seemed that he was beginning to dig under the edge of the tent, I finally decided that at least he wouldn't get me lying down. I flipped out of my sleeping bag and, with a flashlight in one hand and a club in the other, I popped out of the tent. There was one of the biggest porcupines I had ever seen. If I had continued to lie in fright, I would not only have had a bad night, but I would have always thought it was really a bear scratching on my tent. But doing something about the problem was the quickest way to resolve the fear.

All failure begins with fear; success begins with courage. There is a story of a man who was healed by Jesus. Jesus said to him, "Take up your bed and walk," and the man did just that. Probably the reason he hadn't done it sooner was that he was afraid he couldn't, so he didn't try. Jesus gave him the faith to try.

Many of us fail to do the things we really know we should be doing in life, simply because we are afraid to make a venture, to start out. We need to hear again the words that came to the shepherds at Christmastime: "Fear not." And hearing these words, we can say with the shepherds. "Let's go. Let's go to Bethlehem and see." Let's go into a fuller, braver, more exciting life as we trust in God.

Many of the things we fear are very real; they won't just go away. But faith gives us the power to deal with these problems without the paralyzing effect of fear.

Men living in this world without the Christian hope are something like men who are trapped in a mine when there is a cave-in. I remember one mine cave-in. Several men were trapped in the darkness below the ground for a number of days. Finally, rescue teams were able to drill a small hole into the area where the trapped men were. And the first word that came from the men was a question that would come most naturally from anyone in such a situation: "Is there any hope?" And for them there was hope.

In a dark world, where we are trapped by our human weakness, and our own meanness and smallness, and our own mortality, this is the word that comes to our lips when we think long thoughts. Is there any hope? With all the suffering and cruelty and hate in the world, with war and poverty, and greed, is there any hope? And the Christian's faith is a word from God saying: Yes, there is hope. Fear not, I bring you good tidings of great joy.

For we have a Savior who can show us how to live better lives in this world, who can help us have the courage to lay down our lives, knowing that death is not the end, but a new beginning with God. He came to live our life as a man, to suffer our suffering as a man, to die our death as a man in order to overcome our fear as men. Because God cared enough to send his son into the world, we can live without fear.

As individuals we need to remember this; as a nation we need to remember this. Frightened men are dangerous men, and there is too much fear in the world. We need more people who can stand up and say: "The Lord is my light and my salvation. Whom shall I fear? The Lord is the strength of my life. Of whom shall I be afraid?"

The tragedy of race conflict comes from fear. We fear what we do not know, and fear is the father of prejudice. Faith that sets us free from such foolish fear is the only thing that can solve the problem of tension between people of different races and different economic backgrounds. Faith says: Fear not, let us go even now into a deeper fellowship with our neighbors who are a bit different from us.

We talk much these days about civil defense and underground bomb shelters. But it is even more important for us to remember that our final hope in life is not a bomb shelter under the ground, but a star in the sky. Our final faith is not in man-made armament, but in the knowledge that whatever happens, underneath are God's everlasting arms, and under his wings we can safely abide. God, who is our help and our hope, is not far off; he has come to us in Christ. Our worst fears are answered by a great faith.

From Here
to Jackson's
Straw Stack

A few years ago, I was with a group of cattlemen who were having a dispute over the division of their cattle range. It was not a bloody battle like the range wars we see in the Western movies, but it was still a bitter argument. We were on the foothills of a high mountain and a fence was to be built to separate the land allotted to the range users involved. But where to build the fence? That was the question.

Several years prior to the argument, there had been an agreement on the line between the two areas of range. So the notes made at the former meeting were brought out. They said something like this: the range is to be divided by a line running from Ax-Handle Point, a prominent point of rock high on the mountain, to Jackson's straw stack. Jackson had a large ranch in the valley below the disputed range area. But the notes had been made several years earlier and Jackson's ranch was three miles long. Just where had he stacked his straw the year the notes where made? Of course, no one could agree on that. So the argument went on. And the agreement that could have settled the argument was of no use because it had not been based on anything permanent. It was based on a standard fixed to an object that could change with the seasons.

Much confusion, heartbreak, and bitterness is being caused in our society today for a very similar reason—the lack of moral standards that are fixed to eternal truth. Far too often, we guide our lives by fads or fashions that vary with the changing of seasons or generations. If we are going to be sane in what often seems to be a crazy world, we have to have some fixed points of reference for our morals and some definite values to guide us in our search for happiness. Lacking these, we have anarchy not only in our social life but in our own personalities.

We find our lives turning into a rat race. Our days and years are spent in pointless going and coming, like a man lost in the woods who runs around with no notion of the direction in which he should go to find his way home. The fact that we have already fallen into this problem is evident by the number of broken homes, riots, suicides, murders, bankruptcies, and other social evils that have become such a regular part of the news we read and hear daily.

One of the great values of religion is its ability to give people an anchor of stability, a set of values that reaches across generation gaps and does not move around with the changing of fashions. To live a good life, a person needs this stability. An individual in our modern world is like a ship at sea. Everything around him is moving, just as he is moving. Perhaps he is sailing the Gulf Stream, which has a direction of its own. Then the wind pushes from another direction. Unless the ship can get its direction from something above and beyond the immediate situation, it is in real trouble. The ship must not steer by the sea in which it floats but by a star, or a radio beam, or a compass course that has a bearing not changed with the changing sea.

Navigation really began when sailors discovered that the North Star, in relation to earth stays in a fixed position. They had a star to steer by. And progress in the life of a person or a nation really can begin when certain moral and ethical standards are seen to have eternal value, and we see them as something fixed that we can hold onto in time of confusion and turmoil. We must have these eternal points of reference if we are to keep our emotional balance and live good, worthwhile lives. Trying to row a boat across a lake can be very difficult, but if we fix our eyes on some point on the far shore we can make it across in good shape.

We are fortunate in having some definite fixed points in our religious heritage. Our difficulty is that we ignore them. We have such great principles as the Ten Commandments and the Golden Rule. The Ten Commandments are not true because they are in the Bible. They are in the Bible because they are true. They have been tried and found satisfactory by generations for thousands of years. Through all these years, people who have depended on them have lived satisfying lives; people who have ignored them have come to trouble. These great rules have been landmarks like mountain peaks—they have not moved around like Jackson's straw stack.

A person seeking the way to live in a time of confusion cannot afford to ignore guidance of this kind. If we try to guide our actions by the latest article we have read on how to be beautiful, or how to be rich, or how to be popular, without reference to the great landmarks of religion, we may very well be heading for disaster—building on fad rather than fact, on sand rather than on rock.

I read once about a sailor who decided to steer his ship by the reflection of the moon on the water. The reflection of the moon is so pretty, why bother with the North Star that seems so far away? Why bother with a compass that is hard to read and points to a North Pole we can't see anyhow? The moon on the water is so much closer and we know it's there. Why not follow it? This is just about the kind of reasoning that we get from many people today who would rather ignore the great established rules of living and find new and exciting ideas for guiding their lives. It might seem interesting for awhile, but it leads to disaster.

If we have thoughtlessly moved away from the secure markers of our religious faith and find ourselves wandering aimlessly about in life, no effort is too great and no cost too high to get ourselves back in touch with the marker that can keep us from wandering about aimlessly. We do have markers. No matter how mixed up a family might be, it can get back on course with such great truths as: Honor your father and mother. Do not commit adultry. Do not covet your neighbor's wife. Do not bear false witness. Do unto others as you would have others do unto you. No one has ever gone wrong using these markers for guidelines. No matter how mixed up one may be in his business life, he can find his way safely by following, as eternal truth, such guides as: You shall not steal. You shall not lie. You shall not covet.

We run into young people troubled by the amount of cheating that is done in school. It is bad but they say, "Everyone is doing it." Well, everyone isn't doing it. But even if they were, it would not make it right. The majority is not always right; there are some fixed principles that we can depend on regardless of what the majority may be doing. We have always laughed about the mother who watched the marching band and said, "My Johnny is the only one in step." It's just possible she was right. There is just a chance that he was the only one listening to the drumbeat. Right is not always a matter of what the majority is doing.

A man may get lost in the forest if he gets so interested in the things right around him that he forgets to keep track of the great landmarks in the distance. He can lose his life this way. I remember once I was fishing on a beautiful little stream on the Oregon coast. There is lots of rain in that country. The trees are tall and the underbrush is thick. I followed the little stream awhile and then came to a meadow filled with flowers. It was so interesting I walked a good way from the stream and spent quite a bit of time enjoying the various plants and wildlife. The flowers were beautiful and delightful, but when a cloud came over the sun and I realized I should be finding my way out of the forest, I also realized that the flowers wouldn't help me find my way. I had to locate the big old spar tree high on the ridge—the distant tree that marked the place where the trail entered the little valley. Once I got the fixed landmark in sight, I was able to find my way through the underbrush in good order.

Over and over in life we see tragedy and failure because people have fixed their sights on passing fancies, on goals that change with changing generations. They have lost sight of the religious values that have eternal qualities and do not change with

53

the changing seasons. The day we tried to fix the fence line between two areas of range, we very nearly had a fight between good neighbors. There was trouble simply because someone had tried to draw a guideline based on a straw stack that would be gone in a year, rather than fixing the line on some point that would endure through the seasons.

If we are to be sane in a crazy world and live abundant lives even in confusing times, we have to remember that there are eternal mountain peaks we can look to; there are sound laws of surveying that we can use to locate our corners. We don't have to draw our line from here to Jackson's straw stack.

To Catch a Rat

There is a story about a man who lived alone, except for a pack rat. The rat was a constant irritation to the man. Its activities at night kept him from sleeping. It spoiled his food and created a bad smell in his house. He was determined to catch it. But the rat was a very clever rat and would not be trapped. By day it slept quietly, and the man could not locate its hiding place. Finally in a fit of desperation, he set fire to his cabin. He got rid of the rat; he also lost much that was very precious to him. Because of a small irritation, he acted with great foolishness.

How often we let this become the story of our own lives, when some little bother leads to a big mistake. In talking to a couple who were considering divorce (and they did separate) ; I found that the last straw, the incident that triggered the final fight before the divorce action, was fried potatoes for supper. He said he didn't like them; she insisted on serving them.

It is amazing to see how people will come through great adversity with flying colors, only to let some little thing cause big trouble. And one of the most important values of the Christian faith is its power to help us keep things in perspective, so that small irritations will not cause great calamity. There is something infinitely sad about a person being so driven by small annoyances that he burns down his house to catch a rat.

There is a book in the Bible called the Song of Solomon. One rarely reads or hears a sermon preached on a text from this book. Most of the book is simply an old Hebrew love song; it was probably sung at weddings. It has some very lovely passages in which the lovers sing in some detail of their love and attraction for each other. But right in the middle of this love song, a very practical proverb is thrown in. It says: "Catch us the foxes, the little foxes, that spoil the vineyards, for our vineyards are in blossom." (Song of Solomon 2:15 RSV.)

This proverb, coming where it does, seems strange. It is as if you were attending a modern wedding, and someone singing "I Love you Truly" suddenly stopped to make a comment on the importance of joint ownership of bank accounts, or the need for a family budget and careful use of credit. And of course, that might not be a bad idea.

In this old love song the singer sings of the beauty of love. He compares his love to a vineyard in blossom, a vineyard that can, in time, bear sweet fruit. But he also knows that there are things that can destroy a lovely vineyard and that the worst things are the little foxes that can slip in unnoticed and do a great deal of damage. There may be a fence around the vineyard that will keep out big things like cattle. Perhaps a watchtower has been built to keep out thieves and trespassers. But little foxes can come in unnoticed and destroy the blossoms and fruit almost before the owner knows it is happening. So we have this interesting passage, "Catch us the foxes, the little foxes, that spoil the vineyard, for our vineyards are in blossom."

The danger of letting little problems cause big troubles is certainly true in relation to the church. Many people who should be in church, and could be getting strength and help from the church, have left the church for some very petty reasons. I once knew a church where there was a bitter argument over the question of whether to buy a pipe organ or an electric organ. Hard feelings developed over the question of whether to put in carpet or floor tile, as if these things really make much difference in the real meaning of the church. But they were nasty little foxes and they did spoil some blossoms.

All our important relationships in life are endangered by the little foxes. Small irritations can slip into our lives and wear on our nerves and finally cause big trouble if we don't take care of them properly. These small problems are like mice in a bread box. It's not so much what they eat as what they mess up that causes the trouble.

How shall we, as Christians, deal with the small problems that cause big trouble? First of all we need to see that many can be eliminated with a very small amount of effort, if we just take the time to do it. Once I was hiking and had a rock in my boot. I suffered much longer than I should have because I just didn't want to take the time to sit down, unlace my boot, and take out the rock. Some problems are like that. And we should take care of them. If your wife eats crackers in bed, try feeding her before you go to bed. If she snores, try a little cotton in your ears—it can do wonders. I've known families that complained for months about squeaky door hinges, when five minutes with an oilcan would have solved the problem. It sounds simple, but it is amazing how often we let something continue to annoy us when a very little time and effort would take care of it. If there is a way to eliminate the problem, we should quit complaining about it and take care of it.

Many irritations in life are not so simply resolved. They are a part of the things we want in life. Our approach to them should be simply to face the fact they are part of life, and accept them with good humor, recognizing that it is not worth losing a big reward because of a small irritation. Faith can help us with this. We have to face the fact that cars mean traffic problems; gardens mean bugs; children mean spilled milk and jam on the newspaper, sometimes dirt on the towels, and runny noses. But we still like cars and gardens and children. I like to fish, and long ago I decided that fishing some of my favorite spots means putting up with a certain number of mosquito bites.

However, many of our irritations are caused by other people. We could avoid these irritations by avoiding people. But generally speaking, people are much too nice, and being a hermit is a very dull and pointless way to live. So to live among people we put up with some irritations. And as long as we live on earth, and want to enjoy the company of at least a man Friday, or a wife or husband, or children, or neighbors, or friends, we will find some irritations. We will do well to accept them and learn to live with them. Generally speaking, people are pretty nice. They bring us most of the enjoyment that life has to offer.

Not long ago I talked with some folks who had just taken their first trip across central Idaho. It was some of the finest scenery they had ever seen and should have been a great experience for them. But most of it was spoiled for the wife, because on a stretch of road that was not paved, the trailer bounced too much and her aspirin got mixed up with some of the groceries. These things do happen, but we must learn to see the scenery in spite of the annoyances.

Picnics generally mean ants, but I like picnics and I am not willing to give them up because of ants. Homes, churches, dinner parties, families are all much to nice to sacrifice simply because they involve people, even though there are people who do sometimes irritate us and get on our nerves. And if we are going to catch the little foxes that spoil the grapes, we simply have to learn to live above the small irritations. We can do this by keeping our minds on the bigger and better things of life.

All too often when we do let little things get us down, it is an indication of the fact that we are small-minded and have allowed our lives to get too concerned with petty things. I heard about a family that went to another home for dinner some years ago. During the dinner the small son of the visitors was crawling around under the table. He suddenly let out a terrible scream. He had put his finger in a mousetrap. Now if the hostess had been a better housekeeper and kept the crumbs swept up off the floor, it is likely there would have been no need for the mousetrap. On the other hand, if the boy had not been down crawling around on the floor, he wouldn't have been caught in it.

Often the things that irritate us are clues to where our minds are. If the first thing you notice about a restaurant is the gum that is stuck under the table, it might be an indication that you should have your mind on something more interesting. In a world that does have a great many small irritations, we need the words of the great apostle Paul to guide us. "Whatsoever things are true, whatsoever things are honest, whatsoever things are just, pure, lovely, of good report, . . . think on these things." We avoid the small and the petty by having our minds fixed on higher goals.

I never was much of a football player, but I did like the game. In the little bit I played, I know that after a game I could have a number of bruises and never know just when or where I got them. I was too interested in trying to help win the game to be concerned with each bruise and bump. Surely this is the clue to a good life and the way to handle small irritations. We need to be so interested in living and enjoying life that we just don't have time to complain if the coffee is too cool, or the lemonade too warm, or a room a bit too stuffy, or the meat cooked a bit different from the way we like it. No one can afford to burn his house down just to catch a rat.

Switchbacks
on the Trail

This past summer a friend and I made a trip
into a scenic wonderland. On maps and in land
use, this wonderland is known as the Salmon River
Breaks Primitive Area. It lies on the north side
of the Salmon River, in central Idaho, well downstream from the end of a Forest Service motor
road. It is in that part of the river canyon that is

not reached by roads of any kind, only trails. One can get into the area by floating down the river in a boat and then hiking up one of the trails. Or, he can take the main trail that follows the river down to the point where he wishes to climb up into the "breaks" of the canyon, from which the area gets its name.

Since Gene and I were traveling by horse, we took the river trail, leaving our horse trailers at the Corn Creek campground at the end of the road. We traveled down the river for about six miles to the mouth of Horse Creek and turned up Horse Creek for a mile or so. Then we climbed out of the canyon on the Pinto Creek Trail up to the West Horse Ridge, which is the designated east boundary of the Salmon River Breaks.

We made the trip on the excuse that we were looking for a good place to make a fall elk hunt. But we really didn't need any excuse, and we knew it. It is reason enough just to go into such spectacular country. After leaving the river trail, we saw no other people until we returned to the river, three days later. We could relax, listen to the horse bells as our hobbled horses grazed on a mountain meadow in the evening, and imagine ourselves back with the mountain men who used these same trails, with the same basic means of transportation, a century earlier. At that time, the present wilderness was one of the busiest parts of Idaho, as gold seekers, native Indians, pioneer merchants, and adventurers traveled the area with their strings of horses and mules. They were not restricted as we are today, to areas with roads.

In many ways the most interesting part of our trip was the climb up out of the canyon, from the level of the river, which is at an elevation of about three thousand feet at the mouth of Horse Creek, to the site of the old West Horse Forest Lookout, at an elevation of seventy-four hundred feet. The site of the old lookout is actually on the rim of the canyon.

After leaving the river, we climbed steadily for several hours, covering seven or eight miles of trail. In doing this we gained five thousand feet in elevation but not more than two and one half miles laterally away from the river. Looking back toward the river, one gets the feeling that a good ball player could throw a rock from the rim of the canyon back down to the river, a route over which we had spent many hours of hard climbing. On one section of the trail there is a great open face where the trail makes sixteen long switchbacks. This face is so steep that at any point, if a horse were to step off the trail and lose his balance, he could very well roll all the way to the creek bottom where the switchbacks begin. Riding such a trail, it is well to keep in mind the fact that a good horse knows this, has the situation under control, and is safer than a car on a freeway where the "other driver" is not always as dependable as a good mountain horse.

Riding my horse up the Pinto Creek Trail gave

me a good deal of time to think. After getting home I looked up Webster's definition of "switchback." He aptly calls it "a zigzag road in a mountainous region." This almost vertical slope could not be easily climbed without the switchback trail, which was well engineered a number of years ago by the Forest Service. Earlier travelers would have followed a dangerous trail using the natural switchbacks of trails made by wild animals. The long switchbacks on the improved trail keep a good even grade. A horse can keep an even pace as you climb the canyon wall. They certainly zigzag, and if one did not understand the reason for them, the long switchbacks could be most frustrating. I wanted to get to the top of the canyon rim. But after some hard riding, I would find myself looking down at a place just a few feet below my stirrups where I had been many minutes before. One could get to wondering whether or not he was getting nearer his destination. Maybe the trail had a way of going in some sort of weird circle. One would get an urge to try to go straight up the mountain; he could be thankful that his sensible horse did not share the urge.

Riding along on that fine summer day, listening to the steady rhythm of the hoofbeats of my saddle horse and packhorse, feeling the horse's heavy breathing under the saddle, watching Gene and his horses ahead of me on the trail, I thought how much life is like a steep climb up a mountain that can be conquered only by a series of long switchbacks. We set goals that we hope to reach: a good home, a good living, a little money in the bank, better family relationships, a better personality, better education, more self-control—but we don't go right to them. The way is too steep. There are always barriers, and we find ourselves going the long way around.

Like a plane circling to gain altitude, or a sailing ship tacking against the wind, we find our goals in life are reached by a series of long and sometimes very difficult switchbacks. Sometimes we think of them as setbacks. Sometimes we resent them. We want to turn straight up the mountain, or sail right into the wind. And when frustrations get too deep and it seems we are really going nowhere at all, it is important to remember that switchbacks have been put on the trail for a purpose. They may seem to delay us, but they are not on the trail to slow us down; they are there to make it possible to climb an otherwise insurmountable hill. They may seem to hold us back, but without them, we could not climb the mountain at all.

Climbing the Pinto Creek Trail, I thought of some of the switchbacks I have had in my own life—time out for education, financial reverses that taught me some things I needed to know, sickness that has taught patience, just to mention a few major ones. And the Pinto Creek Trail taught me some things about switchbacks that I hope I will always remember. First of all, when you are on a switchback that seems to take forever, remember you really are climbing a little. From time to time, we would stop to rest our horses and let them catch their breath. I could toss a rock into the trail below me where we had been a few minutes earlier. We had not come a long way from that spot, and had not come up much higher, but we had come up a little bit. We were higher on the mountain than we had been—not much, but some. In life this happens. I take a year to complete what I wanted to do in a week. But it is done; I have gained something. I am not actually going in circles. I will not meet myself coming back.

When I feel despair over a twenty-five-year mortgage, and it seems I will never be out of debt, it is important to see what has been paid—to look at my equity and not just the balance due. I need to look down at the switchbacks that are already below me, rather than looking up all the time at the number still to be climbed. I remember a point on the trail when I looked down and saw that we had climbed ten of the sixteen switchbacks. There was a real sense of satisfaction. And in life we need to pause from time to time and be thankful for the gains we have made. Unless one gets some satisfaction from what he has already done on the upward climb, he might lose his mind just thinking about all that he still has to do in the world and in his own life.

The second thing I learned on that trail was to enjoy the view as I went along. I didn't have to wait till we reached the rim to have a fantastic view of the canyon. Each switchback had its own viewpoint, and put the whole canyon in a little different perspective than the view from any other switchback. There were wonderful sights I would never have seen if I could have gone straight to the top—points of view and aspects of the canyon that one cannot see from the top. The exciting views that one gets from the slow progress up the trail reminded me that too often in life we are so eager to get to where we are going that we forget to enjoy the trip. And the journey can often be more interesting than the destination.

I remember a boy whose ambition was to be a retired rancher. Ranching can be a tough life, but the retired rancher who is well-fixed knows that his greatest satisfaction comes not from his financial security, but from remembering the view, the companionship, the struggles, the pain, the long hours in the saddle on the steep trail that he rode to get to the place where he is. Switchbacks can be discouraging, but without them we cannot climb the mountain at all.

Empty Creel

Many of us look forward to the opening day of trout season as eagerly as small children look forward to Christmas. There is something about fishing that has captivated the minds of certain sportsmen for years, and I am one of them. There is more to sport fishing than meets the eye; to truly understand a dedicated fisherman is to understand some great things about life. There is a lot more to fishing than just catching a basketful of fish.

Every real fisherman likes to catch fish. If I were to suggest that I don't like to catch fish when I go fishing, I would be doing some "fisherman exaggeration." In fact, when you hear a person telling about how much better the little trout taste than big ones, it is because he has not been able to catch big trout. But fine as it is to catch fish, in looking back over my own experience, I realize that some of my finest days of fishing have been days when evening came and found me still carrying an empty creel. To me, an empty creel is a symbol of a truth about life.

This spring I took a short trip to fish for steelhead on the Salmon River. I have a friend who operates a jet boat on the river and has a fishing camp several miles down in the canyon where there is no road. The road down the river runs about sixty miles from the town of Salmon, and ends at a Forest Service campground. Below the end of the road is the eighty-mile portion of the river country that has no roads, and is part of the truly primitive area of Idaho. I was to meet Joe at the boat dock at the end of the road in the morning, but I arrived at the end of the road just after dark the night before. It was raining softly, so I had supper and crawled into bed almost as soon as I arrived in the camp. I could hear the soft touch of the rain on the roof of my camper and the powerful surge of the unseen river as it rounded the curve next to the camp. I could think about the day to come—good friends, good scenery, maybe giant steelheads. I could smell the forest around me— great ponderosa pine and the smell of promise there is when gentle warm rain touches thirsty earth. I had a wonderful night of refreshing sleep. Maybe the fact that I was miles and miles from a telephone helped; maybe the sound of the river and the pleasant thoughts of the next day's fishing helped my mind drop some of the problems of my daily work that often interfere with my sleep. But whatever magic may have been at work, a weary mind as well as a tired body had a wonderful rest that night.

Next day we spent on the river, jet boating from one promising hole to another. At this tme of year the steelhead travel upstream. If we fished a good spot for an hour without a strike, we would move to another well-known eddy or stream mouth. The rain the night before had muddied the water just a little; perhaps we used the wrong lures; maybe the moon was in the wrong phase. At any rate we did not catch fish, and a good fisherman can always give a reasonable excuse. Because we were not catching fish—there is a limit of two per day on steelhead trout—we moved around a good deal over a thirty-mile stretch of river. We saw fourteen elk, countless deer, and over a hundred bighorn sheep. We took time for a fine visit with a man in his early eighties, who has lived almost all his life in the roadless part of the Salmon River Canyon. What a pleasure to visit with this man and share his point of view about life. His life has been almost untouched by civilization for the past fifty years. I won't say his point of view is right; I certainly won't say it is wrong. But it is different; it is refreshing. He is thirty years older than I, but there was no "generation gap," just a great sharing of experiences.

We picked up a young man who was walking along the river trail. This young man is about thirty years younger than I am. He had been raised in a large city but had spent the winter in the canyon and was looking for a new way of life. He spent the night in our fishing camp with us. We had a long talk about meanings and problems of life. He was interested in all aspects of wildlife. The next day we checked three different "cougar kills"— the remains of deer killed recently by cougars. Our common interests in the river, wildlife, and fishing spanned our age difference; meeting and sharing with this interesting young man, and finding no "generation gap," enriched my life.

A few years ago I read a delightful book. I have always liked to talk with people who write, but I had never expected to meet the author of this particular book. But with the fishing slow along the river, I took time to visit another fisherman with some time on his hands. It turned out to be the author of that delightful story, *Where the Red Fern Grows*. What a bonus added to a good day on the river.

The Indians that lived in central Idaho until about 1870 used a very interesting system of blazes on trees to mark trails, river crossings, camp sites, and perhaps a number of other things. No one knows much about these blazes, but many of us would like to know more. On this particular fishing trip I found two old trees with Indian blazes, old ponderosa pines that are perhaps four or five hundred years old. I studied the blazes and had time to wonder a little about the men who made them; to reflect on the fact that though we are separated by many years, I have much in common with my unknown brother who stood in the same place, fished the same river, hunted the mountain sheep, and saw beauty in the vastness of the canyon.

Returning home from my fishing trip, I thought how nice it would be if I had a twelve- or fifteen-pound steelhead to brag about, to share with friends. But also running through my mind was the realization of how silly I would be if I thought the fishing trip a failure just because I didn't have a fish. I couldn't escape the fact that I felt very good about a wonderful fishing trip, even though I didn't catch one steelhead. A scripture passage with a little twist to it came to me like this: A man's life is not in the abundance of his possessions but in his possession of abundance. Certainly I had experienced abundance —seeing, hearing, smelling and sharing in the wonder of the world, and finding a closer bond between myself and some of the other men who share the earth with me. Fulfillment is not in just having a lot of things, but in relating with pleasure and appreciation to the things of earth that we do have, without possessing them.

Game departments are doing a fine job of managing our resources. Fisheries that were depleted a few years ago are being restored; polluted streams are being cleaned up. But with all our progress, the number of people who go fishing is increasing faster than the number of fish. In the foreseeable future it will be more and more difficult to catch the limit. It will be more important for the true fisherman to realize that there is still no limit to what he can catch in terms of pure enjoyment of a wonderful sport. I have no quarrel with the person who uses worms, but one thing I like about fishing with a dry fly is the emphasis its puts on the sport and the challenge of fishing. One can have a very full day, even when the shadows of evening fall and find him still carrying an empty creel.

A day last summer I worked a very clear stream. There were some fine fish in it; I saw some of them. They were well-educated—at least on that day I was no match for them. I studied the bugs in the stream. I watched the water. I tried a number of flies. I was resting on a little bridge that spans the stream when a friend drove by. Seeing my empty creel he asked me if I didn't feel just a little silly walking up and down the creek all day with a fly rod, catching nothing. I told him I did feel just a little silly, but not nearly as silly as I would feel if I walked up and down all day without a fly rod. In a sense that fly rod is my ticket to a wonderful relationship with the out-of-doors. I can spend a day wading, like a child wading in rain puddles, for the pure joy of wading in water. Wading around all day without my fly rod might cause some people to think me childish. I can study aquatic insects, watch nesting ducks, see a mother otter teaching her children, look at a hidden, spotted fawn who thinks I can't see him, and, sometimes, catch a very nice fish.

I look back across the years and count over the interesting scenes I have witnessed and the good times I have had, and I am surprised at the number of good things I would have missed if I had not gone fishing. There was the curious yearling doe who, while I stood very still, came up so close I could touch her with the tip of my rod; the black bear, nature's own clown, who fished a riffle just ahead of me one day, and was so intent on his fishing that he didn't see me for a very long time. Bears are good fishermen!

On the farm where I grew up we worked hard. Making a living was not easy for my father. I wish I might have known my father better than I did. We had our problems. But sometimes he took me fishing, and I will never forget the warm, good feeling that would come to me when he would ask me to go fishing with him. He enjoyed fishing, and here was a sharing deeper than words. He's gone now, but I am so thankful for the days in later years when I was able to take him fishing with me.

Happiness is always a by-product of some other effort. If we seek it directly, we always miss it. But we set out after some interesting, worthwhile goal, and suddenly we realize we are happy. Filling a basket with fine trout is a challenge and an obvious goal. You use your skill, your best knowledge, your finest effort, and suddenly you realize you are having a wonderful time even if the basket is not full. Surely life is a good deal like setting out to fish on a fine fresh summer day. Our hopes are high; our goal is a basketful of fish. The day goes along. We may or may not catch the fish we hoped for. We find our plans do not always work out just as we thought they should. But with our eyes open to beauty, our ears tuned to the music of the water and the wind, surrounded with the fragrance of earth, our hearts open to the friendship of our companions, we find when evening comes we've had a very full day—even if we have an empty creel.

High Mountains
in the Distance

During the many years that we lived at Sky
Range Ranch near Salmon, Idaho, we often
traveled the 160 miles to Idaho Falls for business
or pleasure. We traveled State Highway 28, which
takes one from Salmon, up the Lemhi River, over
Gilmore Summit, down Birch Creek, and out across
the vast lava plain on which Birch Creek, Little

Lost River, and Big Lost River all sink into the earth. Most rivers run to the sea, but these great mountain streams simply drop out of sight in the lava formations near the Craters of the Moon on the Snake River Plain.

As you travel State Highway 28 from Salmon to Idaho Falls, after crossing the Gilmore Summit, elevation 7,189 feet, you can look a little south of east and catch sight of what seems at first a vision floating in the sky. You think you cannot possibly be seeing what you think you are seeing, but soon it becomes quite distinct. In the clear mountain air you are seeing, perhaps as much as 125 miles away, the top of the Grand Teton in Wyoming, 13,766 feet above sea level. In the days of the fur trade in the early 1800s, and even in the days of the first settlements in Idaho and Wyoming, this great peak was used as a landmark to guide travelers— travelers who never reached the peak itself, but who found their way across the plains and valleys because they were directed by a mountain peak that was a distant vision, and yet a secure point of reference for everyday travel.

For me, the Christian belief in eternal life is very much like high mountains in the distance. In a sense they are quite remote from my everyday life. Most of my daily work is done without direct reference to the distant peaks. My concern is with the here and now; it must be, as I try to earn a living for my family, make my contributions as a good citizen involved in the struggles and needs of this world. Mine is a worldly religion. God loved the world so much that he sent his Son into it; if God could love this world that much, certainly I should love it too.

The challenges and needs of this world are enough to keep me striving all the days of my life. The neighbors in this world are the ones I must try to love, even if they are as unlovable as I am. As I make my way along the roadway in the valley of everyday life, I do not spend much time gazing at the distant peaks. Sometimes there is just too much smog or dust, and one can't see that far. But the peaks are there. And deep down, in some of my best moments, I know that those distant mountains give my journey a direction and a point of view without which I would get hopelessly lost.

One's point of view can make all the difference between drudgery and adventure. If a person had to spend ten hours a day for ninety days on a treadmill, just putting one foot in front of the other, hour after hour, he might well lose his mind. But when the travelers on the old Oregon Trail plodded along, day after day, just putting one foot in front of the other, it did not drive them crazy. They were not on a treadmill. They were on a journey to a new home beyond the mountains of the West. They had never seen the promise, but they were confident that it held for them something better than what they had known before. So they walked westward day after day, often through hardship and sickness and pain. They walked not as slaves on a treadmill, but as free men with hope. They had seen the high mountains in the distance.

79

My daily effort to be a good person, to be fully human, is enough to keep me busy most of the time. But it is not enough. In the daily struggle to live a good life, I find myself doing the things that I ought not to do, and leaving undone the things that I ought to do. It is then that I need the assurance that there is more to sustain me than just my effort to be fully human. I need to know that the cool stream at which I quench my thirst has its sources high in the everlasting hills of God's mercy. And when the beloved companion who has journeyed with me in the heat of the day, and fought beside me in the battle, and bound up my wounds on the day of defeat, and shared my joy on the day of victory—when this companion who is more than brother, or sister, or father, or mother to me drops out of the ranks, and I pause awhile to make a grave beside the road of life, it is then that I find myself looking far across the valley, far across the flat lands of human weakness, and I lift up my eyes to the vision of distant peaks that promise the life everlasting.

The snowcapped peaks may be barely visible in the mists of morning or in the shadows of evening time; I brush my eyes to be sure that what I see is not a mirage of some kind, caused by looking through tears. But the distant mountains are there, just as real as the ground on which I stand. I can clear the tears from my eyes and continue my journey, assured that at my journey's end I will make it all the way across the valley and enter those mountains and camp in the shelter of their shadow. When the sun is shining, and the day is warm and pleasant, and we are much concerned with the practical, material things of life, it is very easy for us to forget the importance of our great faith in eternal life—a faith that gives us the promise that the presence of God leaves us nothing to fear, even in the valley of the shadow of death.

I remember an evening when my son was eight years old. We were walking together through the forest just at twilight, when the shadows grow long and the stumps begin to look like bears. My son was no stranger to the woods, and he enjoyed camping. But as we walked along, knowing it would be full dark before we reached our camp, he walked very close to me and said with all the honesty of child-hood, "You know, Dad, I'm not afraid of the dark, but I'm glad you are here." As Christians we are not afraid of the dark. But as the shadows fall in the forest I am glad I am not alone. It is good to look across the valley and see that the last rays of the setting sun have touched the snowcapped peaks of the mountains in the distance.

Tall Trees

On a recent hunting trip in the month of October, I saw the tallest aspen trees that I have ever seen. Most aspens grow in little groves or clumps on open hillsides where there is plenty of sunshine; they do not grow very tall. Fifty or sixty feet is tall for a tree in the aspen family. On this particular trip we were packing into country where I had never been before. Our trail led along the edge of a little canyon. The canyon was narrow, and the floor of the canyon was about one hundred feet below the trail. Growing up out of the bottom of the canyon were the most remarkable aspens. They had been protected from wind by the narrowness of the canyon, but they had been forced to compete for sunlight. In their efforts to reach up out of the canyon to catch the life-giving rays of the sun, they had grown extremely tall and graceful. Their slender white trunks lifted their golden leaves up almost level with the trail, high above the bottom of the canyon. The tallness of these trees gave them a remarkable beauty; their struggle to reach as high as possible gave them a character quite different from ordinary aspen trees.

These tall trees are really a thing of beauty. I was amazed to see that they could reach so high. I pondered again the miracle of creation—the ability of plants and animals to adapt to meet the needs forced upon them by environment. Yet for all the wonder of their reaching up, these trees reached only a tiny fragment of the ninety-three million miles to the sun. Their beauty, their life, even their ability to reach up, is made possible by the wonder of the sun reaching down to them.

As we face the constant challenges of the world and seek to live an abundant life, we are constantly reminded that in our human need we, like the trees, keep reaching up for the life-giving warmth of God's love. Certainly our efforts to grow as tall as we can toward him can add beauty and grace.

But we also know that in all our striving we reach only a tiny fraction of the way. Religion is man's effort, reaching up to find God. The Christian gospel is the good news that God, like the warmth of the sun, reaches all the way down to us. His love reaches all the way, coming to us across time, space, and eternity. "The light shines in the darkness, and the darkness has never put it out."

There are two kinds of holidays. There are those like the Fourth of July and Labor Day, that celebrate things that men have done. These are good days, and we enjoy them. But they are quite different from the great days of Christmas and Easter. These are days that celebrate what God has done. They bring us a strange joy that is not in other days. They lift us out of ourselves and give us an awareness of our relationship to him who is greater than we are. As Christmas comes again this year, I will be remembering a bright day in October and the beauty of the tallest aspen trees I ever saw. I will remember trees made beautiful and graceful by their reaching up and up to meet the sun. I will remember the warmth of the autumn sunshine, and the marvel of the sun reaching all the way, ninety-three million miles through space, to touch the trees, to give them life and the ability to grow tall and beautiful. "God so loved the world that he gave. . . ."

Where You Stand

Every fisherman has his favorite lake. Lakes are like friends. It is good to have a number of them, but there will be one that has a special place in your life. With lakes, like friends, I suppose this special quality comes from the experiences that have been shared—good days spent together, the memories associated with that special friend or that certain lake.

The high mountains of Idaho, that area at or above timberline that we speak of as the "crest zone" in land management, has hundreds of fine lakes. Some are quite small, but some are large enough to provide excellent trout fishing. Quite naturally, the best fishing is in the lakes that are hardest to get to—lakes reached by hiking or riding horseback for several miles over steep and sometimes difficult trails. In the best of these lakes, where trout are plentiful, the fish are also temperamental. It can be frustrating to watch fine trout in water so clear you can see the fish easily, and not be able to catch them.

My special lake rests on the lap of a high peak that rises above ten thousand feet; the lake is at an elevation of over eight thousand feet. It is several miles from a road, and they are long, steep miles; but I am very fond of this lake. I have known it for many years and, like a good friend with whom I share fond memories, I will visit it every chance I get.

My first trip to the lake was interesting, but rather disappointing. I had heard of the big trout and the beautiful scenery it offered and, with a friend, hiked to the lake to try my luck. The lakeshore is made up of rock—some in the form of large boulders and some in the form of slide-rock. The lake is very deep, with a surface area of about thirty acres. The steep mountain slopes that make up the shoreline continue their steep slope into the lake, and the water near the shore gets deep so quickly one cannot wade out into the lake. The mountainside is so steep that it makes it very hard to get a good back cast. I did not have a spinning reel. With my fly rod, I found that if a fish was close enough for me to reach him, he was close enough to see me. My "fisherman's luck" was not good. I saw large fish, but after several hours of effort with my fly caught on the mountain behind me, or my line tangled up in an effort to roll cast farther than I was able, I gave up. I left with a few fish and the feeling that the lake was beautiful, but not really very good fishing.

The next trip to the lake was quite different. A friend of mine had some young packhorses he was training, and we decided a trip to the lake would be a good workout for them. Not limited to what we could carry on our backs, we took along overnight camping equipment and an inflatable rubber raft. And what a wonderful trip we had! Fishing from the raft instead of from the steep shoreline made all the difference in the world. Instead of looking at the lake from the shore, I was looking at the shore from the lake. Fish in a lake often feed near the shore because many of the insects they feed on fly into the water from the land. Fishing from the raft, we had the flat surface of the lake behind us for a back cast, and one could place a fly wherever he wished. I have never known better fishing than I had that day, and have had on many pleasant days since, sitting out in the lake on the raft, casting toward the shore, and picking up nice trout within a few feet of the place where I had tried so hard and failed on my first visit.

Many times since first I met my lake, I have had reason to think about it as I have faced other problems in life, some not as pleasant as the problem of trying to catch a big trout. Between my first visit and my second visit the lake didn't change. The trout didn't change. The environment didn't change. What did change was my point of view—my approach to the problem. I changed my position. I changed the place where I stood; I changed myself in order to meet the lake on its own terms, and in so doing, I found a wonderful lake—a fisherman's paradise. Changing myself and my point of view changed everything.

As I visit with people about their problems and hopes, I notice there are basically two ways of looking at life. One way reminds me of my first visit to the lake, where I stood in the wrong place, was frustrated, tangled up, and began to think it was a pretty poor lake. In this position one finds himself blaming the lake, blaming the weather, wondering why someone doesn't do something about planting more fish. It is easy to overlook the all-important fact that he is his own problem because he needs to change his viewpoint. He needs to look at the shore from the lake instead of the lake from the shore.

Then one meets those wonderful people who realize that one can change himself much more easily than he can change the lake, and that where he stands will make all the difference in what he sees and what he catches. This sort of person is willing to see the need for change in himself; he will even seek help in changing himself. I'm sure this is what Jesus had in mind when a well-educated man came to him one night and asked to know more about the way of life Jesus was teaching. Jesus told him he would have to be a new person. The way of life Jesus was teaching was something Nicodemus couldn't see from his old viewpoint. Jesus said in effect: I can't show it to you unless you put yourself into a position where you can see it. But when you are changed, everything will be changed.

Just last spring, on a fishing trip down in the Salmon River Canyon, an interesting thing happened. We had just finished breakfast and were getting ready to go fishing when one of my companions pointed across the canyon at a fine, big ram. But I couldn't see any ram, all I saw was rocks. Finally my friend told me to come and stand where he was standing. Then I sould see it, a magnificent, full-curl ram—one of the greatest sights in nature. But if I hadn't changed my position, I would never have seen it. I might even have thought Joe didn't know the difference between a ram and a rock.

Fly fishing is one of the greatest teachers in the world. Above all it teaches you that what you see depends on where you stand; what you catch depends on where you stand; what you catch depends on how you approach the situation. You approach the stream with the sun in your face, so your shadow doesn't fall on the water and frighten the fish. How easy it is, when we fail to achieve some goal in life, to blame someone or some circumstance, when in fact it was our own shadow that spoiled the picture, our own position that made the achievement impossible. Many times I have returned to my favorite lake—in fact and in memory. Always I remember the difference between my first and second visits; the time when I looked at the lake from the shore, and the time when I looked at the shore from the lake.

It's Your Very Own Moonbeam

When one fishes a dry fly on a lake in summertime, he often finds that the big trout don't start to rise until it is nearly dark. The later it gets, the better the fishing, and if one is not careful he finds himself so intent on his fishing that the time has long past when he said he would be home. If it is a night when a full moon is rising, it is very easy to find that the twilight has been replaced by moonlight. And there is no place on earth more peaceful than a mountain lake on a summer night— a night so still that you can hear the little slurping sound of big trout breaking water.

There are two lights that put me in a reflective mood. One is the light of a campfire as I watch the play of the flames. The other is that soft streamer of light that the moon casts on the surface of a still lake. And the beam of light that the moon casts on the water always comes directly to me. No matter where I stand, no matter where the moon is in the sky, the light on the water is my very own moonbeam. I cannot move to a spot on the shore that will cause the moonbeam I see to point to someone else. And if I have a cabin by the lake, the moonbeam always points to my door, never to my neighbor's door.

Our time puts stress on the phrase, "No man is an island." This is an important truth, and we need to remember it. But we also need to remember that in another sense every man is his own island. In her delightful book, *Island in the Sound,* Hazel Heckman tells of visiting with a woman who had been a longtime resident of Anderson Island in Puget Sound. She quotes her friend: "I guess the island means something different to each of us. I reckon you might say each of us has his own island." How true.

Every man's experience is his own. Ask a city man about his city. You will find every man has his own city. We live in a time of too much crowding. In the United States, eighty percent of the people live on less than two percent of the land. We get in each other's way. We have to learn to live together, and the emphasis on togetherness in our time has its place. But we must not forget that we are individuals. Group efforts succeed only when individuals bring something to the group. Many committee efforts have failed because we put the committee together on the assumption that zero plus zero equals something. It doesn't; not in math, and not in groups. It is important that we learn to care about other people, but before one can care for people he has to be a person. You have to know who you are when no one else is present.

The really great decisions in life have to be personal. You can talk to others and share their wisdom. But the great choices are finally made alone. The decision to be a Christian has to be mine alone. Others can encourage me, but no one can decide for me. The decision to pray has to be mine. Group prayer is good, but it is totally different from personal prayer. When I pray I am on my own island; no one can talk to God for me. When I married I had to decide; no one could make the decision for me. The keeping of my vows is a decision that only I can make. Our relationships with others are all important—love, friendship, togetherness enrich our lives beyond all price. But when God puts a moonbeam on the water it's your very own moonbeam. It will always touch the shore where you stand; you can never make it point to anyone else.

Possum

I have owned several horses. I am fond of horses. Because we use the word "love" for the bond that exists between God and his world, or the relationship between a man and his wife, or a parent and child, one hesitates to say he loves his horses. But what word can we use? It must be stronger than when I say I like my Volkswagen. If you have had a horse that carried you over hundreds of miles of mountain trails, and has brought you back to the ranch in darkness when you could not find the trail, and has been your companion on nights spent in the hills, has worked his heart out for you on a cattle drive, and has never refused to do what you asked, the bond between you and your horse is hard to describe.

Life gives us some hard things to do, things we would never choose to do. But such experiences can give us a deeper understanding of the love and mercy of God. I think God has some things to do that he doesn't like to do. But he has to do them because he is God and he cares.

One of the hardest things I have ever had to do was to take the life of a fine old horse. Possum was a part of our family; he served us well. We bought him for our oldest daughter, Heather, when Heather was nine. Possum was already well along in years, as horse life goes. Heather was soon riding other younger horses in the hard work of working cattle or in the fine riding of a horse show. But because of his dependability, I often found myself taking Possum on a hunting trip to pack game, or to carry a friend who had not done much riding.

My wife, Betty, was not raised around horses, and it was Possum's wonderful disposition and friendly nature that gave her the confidence to ride. He carried her on many very pleasant trips that we have made together into the high mountains. I have no way of knowing how many children learned to ride on him, for he had been a child's favorite for many years before we knew him. After he came to Sky Range Ranch, he was one of the reasons children liked to visit the ranch. Nieces, nephews, neighbors;—there was always room for one more on Possum's back.

He was a strong, agile horse for his age. On a hunting trip he would carry his load all day with the best of the pack string, whether his load was a large man or half an elk. He was proud. To the time of his death he maintained his position as "boss" horse at the ranch, though in later years I suspected that the other horses accepted his domination out of habit and pure respect. I have seen him jump and buck in the pasture just like a younger horse at play, but I never knew him to make an unexpected quick move with a rider on his back. When my wife's mother was in her seventies, she took a ride on Possum while we took pictures. She was not an experienced rider, but I had no fear for her. You could tell by the way Possum walked that he knew he carried a fragile and precious person. I trusted him, and he trusted me.

We vaccinate our horses, and the needle hurts. I have treated Possum for wire cuts. I know a horse cannot understand why we cause him this sort of pain, but I think he knew I would not hurt him just to be hurting him. He never tried to kick or bite or strike. I was never sure of his age, but I think we kept him a little beyond the normal life-span of horses. For Possum's last two years, winter was hard for him. When the ground was frozen he did not exercise enough. Though we gave him special rations and medication, his legs would swell and he was stiff and uncomfortable. The last few days of his life he failed rapidly, and there came the morning when I found him in his favorite place by the creek. He was lying down; the ground was frozen.

It was obvious he could not get up without help. A brief examination made it quite evident that he would not be able to get on his feet again with his own strength. This must be a hard experience for a proud horse that has never refused to do what was required of him. I sat with him awhile, but I knew what I had to do. He was mine. He trusted me do what was right for him. Never would I have willingly harmed that horse. But his age and weakness held him prisoner as no snubbing post or lariat had ever done. I got my rifle, and I set him free. I am not ashamed that tears made it very difficult for me to see clearly to do what I had to do.

An experience of this sort will come back to you many times, and you wonder about your part in it. I did what I had to do because he was mine. I took his life because I loved him and cared for him. If there is a heaven for horses where grass stays green and he can run and play on the hills, I think he still waits for me to come and catch him. And if he saw me coming, he would come running to meet me, even as he did in this life. And when my body wears out, as it will, and there is for me more pain than pleasure in living, the Master that I have learned to trust and tried to serve will take my life. The God who would never willingly hurt me, though he has done some things to me that I could not understand, will give me the gift of death. And I will not be surprised if he does it with tears in his eyes. And he will do it because he loves me, and I am his, and he cares.

A Splash of Gold

In September my daughter and I made a trip from Boise, Idaho, to Sky Range Ranch, near Salmon, Idaho. We were going to get some horses that belong to Heidi. With the horse trailer empty we went the short way through the mountains, a beautiful drive, but on roads that have such sharp curves and steep grades that we don't travel them when we have horses in the trailer. Coming home, we drove the long way around, through Arco, Idaho and across the Craters of the Moon, a vast lava flow that is so raw and bleak that its twisted, pock-marked surface has been named for the surface of the moon. Its geological interest has made it into a national monument that attracts thousands of visitors each year.

We made the trip just after the first frosts had touched the mountains and dressed them in their autumn colors. The aspen trees were at the peak of their color, yet no leaves had fallen. The trip from Boise to Salmon, and most of the trip back home, was through country where the gold of aspens mingled with the green, gray, and brown of ever-greens, sagebrush, and autumn brown grasses to make an almost unbelievable delight of changing colors;—the warm colors of life, colors of joy. Then we came to the Craters of the Moon, somber black rock that lies in great streams and eddies, just as it cooled after flowing from the earth not too many centuries ago. This harsh area is hostile to life, and though it is dramatic and awesome, I have never thought of it as beautiful in the way that a living, green forest is beautiful.

It was with a distinct sense of surprise that my eye caught a splash of gold. I had to look twice, but sure enough, in the ashes of a burned-out crater was a little clump of aspens. How their gold leaves shone in all those miles of black, forbidding rock! They had been there many years, but I had not seen them before; their summer green does not stand out in contrast to the black as sharply as their gold of autumn. And the little grove is small and a long way from the road.

Something about those trees growing in such a hostile environment cheered me. I thought about them the rest of the way home. What a symbol they are for the Christian who faces the challenge of living a good life in a world where there is so much that is hostile to the hopes and ideals of the Christian faith. These little trees are stunted because of the hard situation in which they live. But they do live, and their gold is just as bright as the gold of any aspen tree in the deepest soil or on the most pleasant hillside. Those aspens on the Craters are doing what aspens are called upon to do, not complaining about their harsh environment, but doing everything in their power to live and grow and make the Craters a little better place for other trees and plants in the years to come.

As they cling to life their roots continue to crack the rock, letting in moisture that will freeze and crack the rock some more. Slowly they are making topsoil for future generations of aspens. Each year they produce a crop of leaves that they give back to the earth, and these leaves are adding organic material to the rocky surface, making it possible for more shrubs, flowers and grass to find a footing on the Craters, to add their bit in making the hostile environment a place of life. Each spring and summer as the aspen leaves grow, they make their share of oxygen; they are not complaining about pollution, but to the best of their ability they are

101

curing it. No matter what happens to the rest of the world, the air around that little grove will be a little cleaner and a little better because these trees are alive and doing what God has given them to do.

Seeing these trees in such an unpromising environment lifted my spirits. I thought of the words of Thomas Kepler, who 350 years ago gave us the third planetary law and said he wanted to proclaim the wisdom of the Creator from the works of his creation. Surely God has a message for modern Christians in the creation of the isolated clump of aspen trees on the Craters of the Moon. By all reasonable odds the aspens should simply give up and recognize that theirs is no world for aspen trees. But they do not. They go right on doing what aspen trees must do. They keep cracking rock and adding organic material to make a little topsoil. They purify the air around them, and then, as if they had not done enough, each fall for no obvious or practical reason they add a splash of gold, a bright spot of pure beauty to the somber blackness.

As I go about my daily work, trying to be a Christian in a world where the news is filled with accounts of wars, pollution, overcrowding, racial conflict, and other problems that beset man as a social creature, I keep thinking of those wonderful little aspen trees living in the very heart of a harsh lava flow. It helps me understand what it means to be a Christian. The aspens do not give up, even though their efforts do not make much difference in terms of the hostility of the environment in which they live. They do what they must do because of the nature of aspen trees; the final outcome, in terms of the Craters of the Moon becoming a better place for trees, is really not going to change their action one way or another. It is their nature to make oxygen and purify air; they will go on doing this even if the Craters begin again to pour out sulfur fumes.

It is the nature of being Christian to go on doing one's best to make this a better world. We are not failures if, after we have done our best, the world does not appear any better. We are to love, to give, to care, to forgive even as an aspen tree makes oxygen and topsoil. Whether or not our efforts make a hostile world into a better place is in God's hands. It is just possible that we are living in a time when the world, in terms of war, famine, and pollution, is not getting better. But the Christian, like the aspen, will make his contribution on the side of life.

It is possible that the aspen trees will live and make their contribution to the harsh surface of the Craters at a time when deep beneath the earth some new upheaval, some gigantic eruption, is building up which will once more pour its flaming rock and deadly fumes over the earth's crust. This does not mean that the aspen trees have failed or their lives are futile. They have lived as aspen trees are to live; they have made the contribution that is theirs to make. And to it all they have added a touch of beauty, a splash of gold. Surely here is a parable for the Christian. We may be living, serving, striving, loving at a time when all creation is preparing some great new upheaval that will seem to obliterate our human effort. We may not be. We don't know. The final outcome is with a wisdom far greater than any human wisdom. But we will go on adventuring, sending rootlets into fissures in the hard rock of the world's problems, breaking down barriers, making a little topsoil, making the atmosphere a little sweeter in our homes, our offices, our schools. We will give to life a touch of beauty, a splash of golden light. Those trees give me the faith that God has something going that is bigger than trees or men. An aspen turns gold in a burned-out crater; the light shines in the darkness, and the darkness has never put it out.

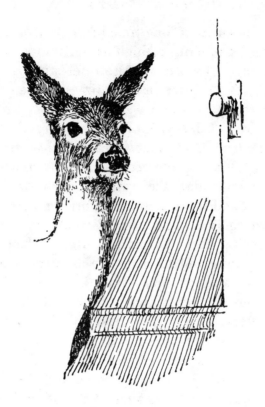

In the Presence
of Enemies

The elk is a prized big game animal in Idaho. The number of hunters who would like to get an elk increases each year; the percent of hunters who do get elk has to decrease. But our game department does an excellent management job. It is remarkable that, in spite of the number of hunters, there are vast areas of Idaho where seasons can remain open for a long time in the fall, and the elk population remains as high as the amount of available forage will permit. Also interesting is the fact that there are three or four times as many elk in Idaho today as there were forty years ago. This is also true of deer. All of this is the result of good management. And many years before the word "ecology" was popularized, the Forest Service, Game Department, and the vast majority of farmers, ranchers, and sportsmen were working on it.

Hunting is a basic part of good game management; being hunted is part of life for the game. It is as fundamental to their life as earning a living is to the average man. But the remarkable fact about the wild creatures is how well they live in the presence of enemies. And this is not just the big game. After years of living in the mountains of Idaho my work has brought me to a home on the very edge of Boise, a thriving, growing city of eighty thousand. I was amazed the other day to see a coyote in our backyard. I knew there were gophers, quail, and pheasants, but a coyote! He was not only surviving but having a wonderful time, just four miles from downtown Boise. In many parts of the United States the white-tailed deer is thriving in close relationship with people.

These wild creatures all look upon man, and rightly so, as an enemy. But they not only coexist with us, they enjoy life. I can find no evidence that gophers get ulcers. On moonlit nights the coyote quarrels with the neighborhood dogs; the pheasants crow with confidence each morning. When we lived on the ranch a deer used to eat the chrysanthemums that grew by our front door, and she showed no signs of being neurotic or maladjusted. These wild creatures seem to know something about life that many modern men have forgotten or never learned. They are wary, but they have a sense of contentment, an assurance, a freedom and serenity that one can envy. Very often I have thought of them when I have reflected on the great words of the Twenty-third Psalm: "He prepares a table before me in the presence of enemies." These wonderful wild creatures know how to partake of that table. Not only do they survive in the presence of enemies, but they have a good time.

The idea of a meal served in the presence of enemies is a fascinating symbol. It means we don't have to have all the problems solved before we can find nourishment for our souls. With God's forgiveness we can find happiness even if there are events in the past that would come back and haunt us if they could. We can live good lives even with physical handicaps that are enemies to our activities.

One of the most important things we need to learn about life, something the wild creatures have learned, is the fact that life is filled with enemies of one kind or another. But life can be good in spite of the enemies, and even in their presence. Anyone trying to do a good job in public life will find enemies, those who disagree with him and try to discredit him. All our enemies don't have to be defeated, all false claims don't have to be disproved. If we trust God and have done our best in his sight, we can come to his table, enjoy the feast, and the enemies can look on if they wish. It would be very interesting if one could know just what had happened in the life of the psalmist which caused him to use this interesting figure of speech. Undoubtedly someone had given him a bad time. Perhaps he had stood up and spoken out for some cause, and there were those who were trying to hurt his character with malicious gossip. Whatever had happened, his was a wonderful confidence that assured him he could live his life, do his job, and in fact have a table prepared with the enemy as a spectator.

As individuals we need this sense of trust and confidence. And as a nation we need to know that we can "come to the table" in the presence of enemies. We hope and pray for peace with all men; but we know that if living the abundant life has to wait until there is political peace on earth, we will never live the abundant life. All indications point to the fact that in this world, because of misunderstanding, greed, jealousy, or some other reason, there will always be some enemies who would harm us if they could.

As individuals we are surrounded by enemies of another sort, enemies such as heart disease, old age, arthritis, cancer. As we grow older we are all too aware of the old truth that each hour wounds us and the last one kills. But the glory of the Christian life is that it can be lived and enjoyed, even in the presence of these well-known enemies. I knew an old coyote that lived several happy, adventure-filled years right under the nose of a trapper who was trying to get him. I know a wonderful man who is living a great life with a disease that he knows will finally take him. But each new day he sits down with joy at the table prepared for him in the presence of his old enemy, death.

Some of the worst enemies we have are our nerves and emotions. Feelings of inferiority, bashfulness, fear of people—these can be very real enemies. Faith can teach us to live in their presence. We face difficult personal relationships in our work, difficult family situations, tension on overcrowded highways —the list is endless. And in those rare moments when I have a chance to watch an elk or deer, a coyote or fox, and see his pure enjoyment of life, I think of one who said we should be not anxious. His was the confidence and joy that come from knowing a table is spread, even in the presence of enemies.

Jet Boat Fishing

For about eighty miles the Salmon River runs through a canyon where there are no roads. This stretch of the river provides some fine fishing for the great oceangoing steelhead trout. They generally weigh from five to twenty pounds. We realists know that with the increasing number of fishermen, the chance of catching a steelhead becomes less each year, and the man-hours of fishing, per fish caught, increases. Maybe that's the reason a steelhead is such a prize, the reason we see it more and more as a trophy fish. Getting a steelhead is a real challenge for the fisherman. However you look at it, if you've ever caught a steelhead you will try again if you get a chance.

The main source of transportation on the roadless stretch of the Salmon is the jet boat. Using Newton's third law of motion, the same principle used to send a rocket to the moon, the boat is driven by thrust from a jet of water. Drawing only three or four inches of water, with no propeller or rudder to be endangered on rocks, and with power to go upstream against tremendous rapids, the jet boat is ideal on the river. It adds real adventure and flexibility to a fishing trip. The shoreline of the river is made up of huge boulders with an occasional sandbar. Fishing is done from the shore; you stand on a big rock, or sandbar, or, in early spring, a large chunk of shore ice. The secret of success is to know which rock to stand on. The fish are in the process of moving upstream in their annual spawning migration.

A hole by a certain rock that has fish in it today might not have another fish in it for several days. To improve our chances of being in the right place at the right time, we like to fish one hole for awhile, then if we don't get a strike in half an hour or so, jet down the river for a few miles to another likely spot. If the fishing is slow, your jet boat pilot may put you out at a number of places

111

over a thirty- or forty-mile stretch of the river in the course of a day's fishing.

Catching a steelhead is a real thrill. They feed on the bottom of the river, and you have to let your bait bump along the bottom if you are to get it where the fish are. But this means being very careful not to get your outfit caught in the rocks. One can lose quite a bit of gear, but with practice many hang-ups can be avoided. A special sinker with little fingers of wire to keep it from getting into tight places between rocks has been developed and is a great help.

Steelhead do not strike hard, and much success is due to being sensitive enough to know the difference between the feeling that comes through your line when a steelhead is mouthing the bait and the feeling that comes from the sinker bumping the bottom of the river as the current washes it along. I am sure that many fishermen have failed to get steelhead because they have been unaware of the fact that a fish was checking out their lure.

The more I fish, the more I am sure that there is about the same element of luck in fishing as there is in almost all other interesting and worthwhile activities in life. Opportunity knocks, but the interesting and worthwhile opportunity knocks softly. Success is to the sensitive. Of all the fish I have fished for and caught, the steelhead is the most cautious in his approach to a bait or lure. He takes it gingerly, but when hooked he is a giant. The beginner may have a steelhead bite but never know it. Thinking it is just another bump on the bottom of the river, he fails to set his hook, and the fish goes on about his business. Or the beginner will lose a great deal of expensive tackle by snagging on the bottom, simply because he overreacts. Every time his sinker hits a rock he tries to set the hook. All too often he gets the job done with the hook or sinker firmly set in a crevice between sunken rocks. Like so many things in life, catching a steelhead is a matter of combining some luck with a great deal of doing the right thing at the right time.

To be in the right place at the right time is the real challenge for the fishing guide who operates a jet boat. The jet boat gives flexibility and makes it so one does not have to spend all day in an unproductive spot. But it also gives the temptation to travel about so much that you never seriously work out all the possibilities. It seems to me that our boat style of fishing is a lesson of life. When should you travel, and when should you sit? Certainly if you travel too much, you may be leaving a fine big eddy just when a school of fish is moving into it. And if you get stubborn and stay on one rock all day, it might just be that no fish will be along that spot for another day or so. I have noticed that the successful old-time fishermen and the able fishing guides have developed a keen sense of when to concentrate on a hole and when to move on to more promising waters. They are not always right, but their percentages are so much better than the average that I'm sure they have

113

learned that there is a time to go and a time to stay.

We all face this question from time to time in terms of success and satisfaction in our lifework. We grow up and get into a job. It is like picking a good rock to fish from. We work hard for awhile. Maybe we get a strike, and maybe we don't. But our modern way of life is a good deal like fishing with a jet boat to move us about. We are not stuck on one rock nearly as much as our grandfathers were. Certainly one doesn't want to be fickle and move about just to be moving, or he will find he is having a boat ride, which is fun, but not catching any fish.

But certainly in our time the person of faith will have confidence in himself and know that if he is in an unproductive situation and is not finding the reward and opportunity that life can give, he can jet down the river, and even if the day is well spent he may find an exciting new situation where the fish are biting. I like to think of life as a jet boat fishing trip. If the fish are not biting in one place, you can jet off to another. I don't ever plan to retire. I'm just going to jet down the river to a big eddy that I have never had time to fish before, and it might be that I will catch the biggest steelhead I've ever caught in my life.

It Was There All the Time

Fishing in a high mountain lake, many miles from a road, can be one of the finest experiences that a fisherman can have. Certainly the isolation of the lake, the fact that one might very well share it with few other fishermen—and maybe no one but members of his own party—adds to the pleasure. To

115

find this sort of isolation means going to lakes that are hard to get to, lakes that are reached by trails that are steep enough to discourage most hikers. Certainly one will not find isolation near a road, or even where one can go with a trail bike.

A boat or raft of some sort adds a great deal to the enjoyment of lake fishing. It is much easier to cast a fly if one is not worried about his back cast catching a bush or a rock. And generally the natural drift of a raft is just right for moving about the lake. If there is a little breeze, fly fishing can be about perfect from a raft that is just drifting with the breeze.

The very remoteness that makes many lakes a real pleasure also presents a problem in terms of getting to the lake with a boat. I remember years ago I carried a rather light canoe about two miles to a lake, but the trail was not too steep. Carrying a canoe into the lakes I have enjoyed the past few years would be impossible, or nearly so. I can remember in years past trying to make a raft of some sort. But high lakes are often in areas where there is very little timber, and some of the efforts at raft-building were pretty frustrating. Always I was wishing for some material that would make a satisfactory raft, and never did I find much that was satisfactory. Then the problem was solved with something so simple we wonder why we didn't think of it sooner.

With the development of the life raft for flyers during the Second World War, there came the lightweight, inflatable raft for use by sportsmen.

The raft I use now weighs no more than my tent. It folds up into a compact bundle that fits into a feed sack and can be added to the load on my pack-horse without any difficulty. Whether it's five or fifteen miles to the lake, having a satisfactory raft when I get there is no problem. And as I float around in comfort, and reach fishing spots I could only have dreamed about before, I think how really simple it all is. The material needed for a raft, the material that is light and will hold me up, is air. And it was there at the lake all the time. All I needed to do was bring a bag to put it in. The little four-man raft that I have at present—obviously made by very small men, but it does accommodate two men very well—is simply a container, a way of making use of the material that has always been available.

So often in life when we are confronted with a problem, the resource we need for solving the problem is so close we don't even see it or think about it. Our problems are generally solved by learning to use what has been there all the time.

Most of us who have difficulty getting along with other people will find, if we really search, the resources we need for being more friendly, thoughtful, and understanding right within ourselves. We need a bag to put it all in, a deliberate concentrating of our best qualities into a way of life that is neighborly. And it can be done. It takes some effort, just like pumping air into my rubber raft. And the wonderful part of it all is that you don't have to search very far for the love and goodwill that is needed. Like the air, it was there all the time, and will continue to be available as needed. And it will hold us up and get us to some places we could only have dreamed about before.

Patient Pack Mule

There is a point of rock along a canyon trail on the Middle Fork of the Salmon River where it has been necessary to blast out a notch in the rock to accommodate the trail. The canyon wall is so steep that there is no other way to get around this solid rock barrier. The trail goes through what amounts to a tunnel that is open on one side, or you could say it just goes under a rock overhang. The trail has been improved in later years, but there used to be very limited clearance for a pack animal. A high pack often scraped the rock ceiling. If an animal panicked and jumped off the trail, it would certainly be disastrous. At this point on the trail there is a vertical drop of over one hundred feet into the river below.

A number of years ago some men were using this trail to pack material to a bridge construction job, where a pack bridge was being built across the Middle Fork. On a trusted pack mule, on top of his regular pack, they had a wheelbarrow. Upside-down it made a good top pack, but it did ride high. With the wheel to the front it sloped up toward the back. Before they realized what had happened they found their mule literally wedged in under the overhanging rock. Many animals, finding themselves trapped in this way, would have plunged off the trail. But the fine old mule showed his quality as a pack animal, a quality that is much prized in mules. He recognized his bad situation, and simply stopped and waited until the young men could secure the rest of their animals and carefully work the pack off the mule to free him. One jump from the mule during this process could have been fatal for him, and might have pushed the packer over the edge to his death as well. But the instinctive wisdom of a good pack mule saved the situation. Sensing that his efforts could only make matters worse, he waited patiently for his master to help him safely through his predicament.

The quality of patience in an unexpected and dangerous situation is a quality that packers prize in mules. It is sometimes found in a horse, but not often. Too often in a tight, frightening situation a horse will try to free himself by plunging and jerking. Many horses have been lost and men killed or injured on bad trails because of this panic reaction to danger.

In life we all find ourselves traveling dangerous trails of one sort or another. It is easy to be caught in a situation that is not of our making and certainly not to our liking. And all too often our first reaction is to strike out, to plunge, to kick, to fight. By doing so we not only endanger ourselves but anyone who would try to help us. I remember a horse I was leading with all my camp gear packed on him. I led him under a large, leaning tree that had fallen across the trail. I thought the pack would clear the tree, but it caught. The moment the horse felt the bind of it he bucked. In this case no one was hurt, and the worst result was a jar of sourdough smashed inside my bedroll where I had put it to keep it from freezing.

When life puts us in a bind and it seems we are trapped and there is no way out, we will do well to have the wisdom of the old pack mule. He has learned to stop, and wait, and be helped. He has learned that the one who leads him can help him out of bad situations that he cannot work out by himself, and often cannot even understand. And he has learned that this help does come when he waits with patience for it.

It's Upstream
All the Way

There are a number of places in central Idaho where one can watch, in the clear water of a mountain stream, the magnificent Chinook Salmon on its spawning bed. One such place, on the upper Salmon River, is right beside Highway 93, and a special turnout and parking place has been provided for the tourist to stop and watch this remarkable scene. Here is a fish that started life near this very spot, several years before. Her mother deposited eggs in the gravel stream bed, and the fish hatched from an egg no larger than a small pea. She emerged from the gravel, and as she grew she worked her way downstream: down the rapids of the Salmon River for three hundred miles, to the broad and powerful Snake River, down many miles of the Snake to the mighty Columbia, and than at last, resembling a good-sized trout, she moved out into the great stretches of the Pacific Ocean to spend most of her life. Here food is abundant, and she grew to be a great fish, perhaps forty inches long and weighing as much as forty or fifty pounds.

During her life in the ocean she traveled countless hundreds of miles, explored icebergs and undersides of ships, perhaps swam beside a submarine. And then one day a strange miracle began. An urge beyond her understanding started her back toward the spawning bed, high in the mountains of central Idaho. From far out at sea she came, without compass, or radar, or periscope, but with an unerring sense of direction, back to the mouth of the Columbia River. How did she do it? Who knows? Had she been spawned in a branch of another river, to another river she would return. But she is a Salmon River fish, so it is to the upper Salmon River, a thousand miles away, that she turned her course. From hundreds of miles of coastline she picked the mouth of the Columbia River. At the junction of the Snake and the Columbia, it would be just as simple to continue on up the Columbia and into Canada as to pick out the waters of the Snake. But with an uncanny sense of direction she came up the Snake to its junction with the Salmon and there again made the proper choice. She turned her course up the swift-flowing Salmon to climb its rapids and spend her stored energy climbing over a mile in elevation to that spot of cool clear water where she began her life. This is where she will deposit her eggs to keep the amazing cycle of life moving as it has for unknown generations of her kind.

The last, final climb up the river required all her strength. It is uphill all the way. But nothing will turn her back. There is no record, as far as I know, of any salmon ever facing the rapids, deciding they are too swift, and turning back for a more comfortable life in the calm of the sea. The long, uphill swim will use her strength. She will lay her eggs and die soon afterward. But she will have completed the course that is hers to complete. She will have attained her goal and finished what was hers to do.

There are many spawning beds for salmon in the Salmon River and in many of its tributaries. Often when I have been fishing for trout, I have seen a great salmon slowly working the gravel with her tail, preparing the place for her eggs, guarding her nest from lesser fish that would eat the eggs as she lays them. And never can I resist the urge to simply stand and watch and wonder as this great fish goes through this age-old ritual that marks the successful ending of her life purpose. Her very presence in the high mountain stream is living proof that she has faced amazing hazards and come through them successfully.

I have often wondered just why it is that to fulfill her life purpose the salmon must have such an uphill struggle. Maybe it is some law of survival, some principle that wills that only the strong and the determined shall be the parents of the next generation. I do not know the answer. From the point of view of the soft and comfortable life that most of us yearn for, it seems there is no good reason for the salmon to struggle so hard. She could swim to the sandy beach of the ocean and lay her eggs in the sand without the terrible ordeal and the body-bruising trip up the hundreds of miles of swift water to her ancestral home. But a wise Creator has ordained that she, and her kind after her, will struggle upstream to reach their spawning ground. And upstream they come—upstream all the way, or die trying.

For some good reason God has given to us all a life that is somewhat like the struggle faced by the salmon. Worthwhile projects, truly rewarding achievements that capture our interest and demand our best, always turn out to be upstream business. Invariably there are rapids that block our way and demand strength almost beyond endurance in the achievement of any tasks that bring real satisfaction. If we try to plan a life that avoids struggle, and always does things the easy way, and seeks a sandy beach rather than a long, upstream battle with the current, life loses its zest and we find ourselves questioning our very purpose and being. As I look at life—the task of being a good father and husband in a society filled with social problem, the task of doing my work well in my profession in a world filled with irritating people and frustrating problems, the challenge to be a Christian citizen in a world with war and poverty and prejudice—it seems there is always a current pulling against me. It's upstream all the way.

There are times when I want to cry out to God and say: Why must it always be such a struggle? Then I think of the magnificent Chinook Salmon, in many ways the fish that I consider the greatest of all fish, and I'm sure that in some very important way it is the upstream struggle that makes the salmon a great fish. I think of the apostle Paul, who rejoiced in a life in which he was beaten with rods, shipwrecked, and stoned, yet achieved a sense of satisfaction that few of us achieve and came to the end saying, I've fought the good fight and run the race, and I press on toward the goal, upstream all the way. When I see a great salmon leaping over the rapids and pitting her strength against the downstream thrust of the river, I realize it is the struggle that makes it all worthwhile. Take away the struggle and you have a carp, not a salmon. Without a battle there is no victory; without a challenge there is no life.

DON IAN SMITH is a man who knows and loves the country about which he writes. He was pastor of the Salmon United Methodist Church for more than fifteen years and for many years owned, lived on, and operated a small cattle ranch near Salmon, Idaho. Later he was pastor of the Hillview United Methodist Church in Boise, Idaho until his retirement in 1983.

Mr. Smith is a graduate of Willamette University in Salem, Oregon, and Garrett Theological Seminary in Evanston, Illinois. His experiences as a pastor, rancher, parent and outdoorsman have furnished inspiration for this and his other books, *By the River of No Return* and *Sagebrush Seed*.